Chapter 1
The Making of
the Time-Tables

When the 20th century opened, there were six great
powers in Europe. They were, in alphabetical order,
Austria-Hungary, France, Germany, Great Britain or
more accurately the British Empire, Italy, and Russia.
Though they were not equally powerful, even the least of
them — probably Italy — was decisively stronger than the
most considerable of the powers in the middle rank. Russia was the greatest in population; Great Britain the
greatest in financial resources; Germany the greatest in
economic strength, with Great Britain not far behind.
There had been no war between any of these great powers
since the Franco-German war of 1870-71. There had been
disputes between them, usually over questions outside
Europe. Threats had been exchanged, but there had been
no serious mobilisation of rival forces since the conflict
between Russia and Great Britain over Constantinople
in 1878 had brought the two powers close to war.

This remarkable run of peace had been achieved virtually without formal organization. The Concert of Europe
was a phrase, not an institution, and even as a phrase had
not much reality. The powers maintained ambassadors at
one another's capitals, and ambassadors and foreign
ministers talked together at length, sometimes amicably,
sometimes the reverse. The crowned heads, who still had
a large say in determining policy, were all personally
acquainted and even included the President of the French
Republic, a little condescendingly, in their social rounds.
Apart from this, there were few international meetings.
The great exception was the Congress of Berlin in 1878,
but even this, unlike earlier congresses, discussed few
general questions and was content to revise the peace
treaty which Russia had imposed on Turkey earlier in the
year. There was a conference at Berlin in 1884 over central Africa and another at Algeciras in 1906 over Morocco.
During the Balkan wars, the ambassadors in London met
regularly under the chairmanship of Sir Edward Grey,
the British foreign secretary, in order to ensure that they

*Left: A premonition of disaster, Spring 1913 asks timidly: 'Will
the god of war crush the flowers this year with his iron foot?'*

were not dragged into war by the doings of the belligerents. For most of the time, however, international relations seemed to run themselves.

In this liberal age, men came to assume that political relations between states, like economic relations between individuals, were governed by a beneficent law of nature, and that if each state, like each individual, pursued its own interests, the good of all would be achieved. In international affairs there was a special law, known as the balance of power. This, too, was supposed to be self-operating. An unknown Providence ensured that, if one power became too strong, the others would automatically shift their weight, without knowing what they were doing, and the balance would thus be safely restored.

The civilisation of the later 19th century rested on the belief that certainty, and therefore security, could be indefinitely prolonged into the future. The most obvious example of this was the railway time-table. With its aid, a man could state, down to the minute, precisely where he would be a month or a year from now. Similarly, an investor would lay out his money in government bonds, with the absolute confidence that these would retain their full value for fifty or a hundred years ahead. In England landowners granted leases for 99 or even 999 years, equally confident that society and money would remain exactly the same throughout that time. International relations operated under the same expectations. Statesmen drew up arrangements with each other which were to last for an indefinite future. These arrangements produced the system of alliances which seemed to shape the politics of the early 20th century.

The system had been there so long that it was treated as though it had been there for ever. In fact, like so many traditions, it was of 19th-century invention. Statesmen had of course referred to their 'allies' for generations past. All they meant was a vague friendship towards the allied country and perhaps a hope that they might work together in time of war. Alliances, in the form of precise written engagements, were made only in wartime or when a war was about to break out, and they dissolved into generalities when the particular war was over. Bismarck inaugurated the new system when he made a peacetime alliance with Austria-Hungary in 1879. Ironically, the inventor of the system did not like it. He included a clause that the alliance was to last for five years, unless renewed. He added that every alliance included the unwritten clause, *rebus sic stantibus* — as long as things

Left: The crowned heads of Europe were a big happy family mainly descended from Queen Victoria. But this did not mean that they got together to keep the peace as this cartoonist hoped

7

remain the same. However, his successors did not follow his maxim, and the Austro-German alliance was generally assumed to have become a fixture in the international law of Europe. The provisions of the alliance were simple. If either party were attacked by Russia, the other would come to its aid; in any other war (most probably a war between Germany and France) the second ally would remain neutral.

In 1882 Bismarck also brought Italy into his system which thus became the Triple Alliance. This too was simple. Germany and Italy would aid each other in case France attacked either; Italy would remain neutral if either of her allies were at war with Russia. Other clauses of a more temporary nature were tacked on as the years went by, but essentially the Triple Alliance remained the same. Few people, however, took it very seriously. Italy had laid down the condition that she would not go against Great Britain and therefore moved away from her Triple Alliance partners when Great Britain was reconciled with France. Moreover Italy and Austria-Hungary were on bad terms. Italy coveted Austrian territory, and Austrian generals often pined for a war against Italy, the only war which they were likely to win.

The alliances spread

Bismarck's system was designed to provide security against the supposedly aggressive powers, France and Russia. These two were, however, equally apprehensive of an attack by Germany and after many hesitations concluded an alliance on their side in 1894. Oddly enough there was no precise political agreement, only a military convention. This provided that at least a third of the Russian army would act against Germany, if Germany attacked France. It also provided that France would mobilise, though not necessarily go to war, if Austria-Hungary did so. Strangest of all, the convention was to last as long as the Triple Alliance, though neither France nor Russia knew the latter's terms. This last provision was cancelled in 1899.

There were other alliances between great powers and lesser ones: an Austro-German alliance with Rumania, for example, directed against a Russian attack; a British alliance of long standing with Portugal; and three general treaties of guarantee, involving all the great powers, for the benefit of Switzerland, Belgium, and, more vaguely, Luxembourg. Outside Europe there was an alliance between Great Britain and Japan, by which after 1905 each promised to aid the other in the event of attack by any one power. After 1911 this alliance did not apply against the United States. But all these were extras. The essential European balance was between the Franco-Russian or

Dual Alliance on the one side and the Triple Alliance, or more realistically the Austro-German Alliance, on the other. Both sets of alliances were strictly defensive if taken literally: they were to operate only in case of attack, and since every great power declared that it was exclusively concerned with defence, war was theoretically impossible.

The great powers had comparatively few direct causes of conflict with each other. Germany did not desire any additional territory in Europe: neither the Baltic Germans nor the Austrian Germans interested her. France would seek to recover Alsace and Lorraine if war came about, but most Frenchmen agreed that they would not start a war to recover them. Russia would have liked to control Constantinople and the Straits, but was reasonably content so long as no other great power did so. Some Austrian militarists had fantasies of recovering the Italian lands which had been lost in 1859 and 1866, but these fantasies had no reality. Many Italians wished more urgently to liberate the irredentas of South Tyrol and Trieste, but they lacked the strength to do it.

Conflict could, however, arise by accident or from questions, apparently trivial and remote from Europe. Great Britain and France nearly went to war over Siam in 1893 and over the upper Nile in 1898. Germany and France got fairly close to war over Morocco in 1905 and 1911. Russia and Great Britain had repeated alarms – over the Near East, over Persia, over Afghanistan, and over the Far East. Russia and Austria-Hungary had alarms over the Balkans – at first over Bulgaria and later over Serbia. These conflicts often threatened to bring the alliances into play. For example, if Russia attacked Austria-Hungary as the result of a quarrel over Bulgaria, would Germany be obliged to aid Austria-Hungary, as she had undertaken to do in the Austro-German alliance? Or if Germany attacked France as the result of a quarrel over Morocco, would Russia have to fulfil her promise under the Franco-Russian alliance? On the whole, the various powers rejected such consequences. An attack which brought the conditions of the alliance into play would really have to be 'unprovoked aggression', in the later 20th-century phrase. Thus Bismarck steadfastly refused to promise support for Austria-Hungary in the Bulgarian troubles during the 1880s. If she wanted to oppose Russia, he said, she must find other allies – Great Britain and Italy. Later, Russia refused to support France in the two Moroccan crises of 1905 and 1911. France refused to support Russia in the Bosnian crisis of 1908.

Left: Bismarck, the architect of the alliance system; he never meant the Austro-German alliance to become a permanent fixture

In ordinary day-to-day affairs, the precise written alliances seemed to count for comparatively little and were no more than a last resource. What really mattered were vaguer unwritten associations of the old sort. Here again the main groups were the same: Triple Alliance against Dual Alliance. But there were many exceptions to this generalisation. France, for instance, was of all the powers the most opposed to the establishment of Russian control over Constantinople and the Straits and, while she gave a vague approval to Russia's ambitions in the Far East, did so only in order to divert Russian interest from the Near East. On the other side, though German and Austro-Hungarian interests did not conflict, they did not coincide. Germany cared little or nothing for the Balkans, which were Austria-Hungary's sole preoccupation. Austria-Hungary was totally aloof from Germany's world policy of a great navy and colonial acquisitions.

Great Britain stands aloof

Great Britain always refused to make any binding alliance in peacetime, except for the historical relic of her alliance with Portugal. But she played an active part in the vaguer understandings. After all, friendships, if not alliances, were needed for many lesser purposes than war — particularly for such things as the international supervision of finance in the derelict empires, Turkey, China, and Egypt. At one time Great Britain co-operated with Austria-Hungary and Italy against Russia in regard to Turkey. She co-operated with Germany and Italy against France in regard to Egypt. She tried unsuccessfully to co-operate with Germany against Russia in regard to China. Later she made up her quarrels with both France and Russia in agreements known as ententes. Were these ententes merely settlements of differences, as they claimed to be? Or did they imply a more general partnership? Sometimes the one, and sometimes the other. After 1904, when the Anglo-French entente was made, Great Britain was always on good terms with France and was even ready to say that the maintenance of French independence was an important British interest. But she gave no firm promise of military support. With Russia, Great Britain was often on cool terms even after making the Anglo-Russian entente in 1907, and she certainly did not declare that the maintenance of Russia as a great power was vital to her. **15 ▷**

*Near right: Edward VII plants a tree to commemorate the signing of the Entente Cordiale and cements the new friendship between France and Britain. **Top right**: The new companions, the Anglo-Japanese Alliance. **Bottom right**: Difficulties at the Hague Peace Conference of 1907. Peace: 'Won't you let me trim your claws?' German eagle: 'Thanks, I prefer them long!'*

The Dress Rehearsal which was ignored

The Russo-Japanese war was the only large-scale experience of war by the great powers since 1878. It showed all the characteristics which were later to distinguish the First World War itself: trench warfare, useless slaughter, incompetence of command, the Christian god transformed into the god of war, and finally a revolution in the defeated country. Foreign observers attended the battlefront. General staffs wrote ponderous studies of the war. But no one drew lessons of any value. No one commented on the prolonged deadlock of the trenches. No one remarked that the mass armies made a war of movement impossible. No one noticed the futility of trying to use cavalry against machine-guns. Ironically it was the two belligerent powers Russia and Japan which soon afterwards formed a partnership to exclude all other powers from the exploitation of China. **Below:** Russian cavalry unload their horses from a train. **Right:** Russian forces advancing during the early stages of the war before the long and arduous stalemate of the sieges had begun

Though all the powers relied on the alliances for their security and power, they relied even more essentially on their own strength. After all, they were no good as allies unless they were strong. The strength of the continental powers took a common form. All had vast armies composed mainly of infantry and based on universal military service. This system had been adopted by all the great powers, and most small ones also, after Germany's victories in the Franco-German war. In theory, every young man received intensive military training for either two or three years and remained liable for recall for some years thereafter. Then he was placed in the reserve, and these reservists, in the judgement of all military authorities except the German, were not fit for war until they had received a new period of training. The system was by no means watertight. In most countries, those proceeding to a university or to other higher education got off with one year's military service, and in countries with more population than industrial resources, such as Russia, many men escaped without serious training of any kind. Still, every country could count on having some millions of men under arms within a few weeks of the outbreak of war.

This was the great operation known as mobilisation. At a given signal — usually the display of placards on public notice-boards — every man recently discharged would proceed to rejoin his unit at a centre designated on his card. These units would in turn proceed to some higher formation until the structure of armies was complete. Not only would men be on the move. The light and heavy guns and their shells had also to be assembled from their peace-time parks. Most conspicuous of all would be the horses, most of them also mobilised from their peacetime tasks. Quite apart from the cavalry and their remounts, there would be horses for the artillery and their supply wagons, horses to transport everything needed by the infantry from first-aid stations to field kitchens, and, above all, horses by which officers could carry messages or direct the march of their men. Every railway wagon in France had long been labelled: '40 men or 8 horses', and the wagons in other countries bore similar designations. The entire process would be conducted by rail, until the armies had reached the assumed point of battle, and general staffs had been labouring for years past to perfect their time-tables. It was universal doctrine that speed was essential. Whichever power completed its mobilisation first would strike first and might even win the war before the other side was ready. Hence the time-tables became ever more ingenious and ever more complicated.

Left: The railways in action. Bulgarian troops on the way to the siege of Adrianople during the Balkan wars against the Turks

15

Major-General Sir Edward Spears, who himself watched the French mobilisation in August 1914, has left a classic account of the problems involved:

If the mobilisation is delayed or slow, the enemy will be enabled to advance with a fully equipped army against an unprepared one, which would be disastrous.

The time factor also makes it essential that the armies, once mobilised, should find themselves exactly where they can at once take up the role assigned to them. There is no opportunity for extensive manoeuvres: mobilisation is in itself a manoeuvre at the end of which the armies must be ready to strike according to the pre-arranged plan.

The plan is therefore obviously of vital importance. It has of necessity to be somewhat rigid, for it has to be worked out in every detail beforehand. From the moment mobilisation is ordered, every man must know where he has to join, and must get there in a given time. Each unit, once complete and fully equipped, must be ready to proceed on a given day at the appointed hour to a pre-arranged destination in a train awaiting it, which in its turn must move according to a carefully prepared railway scheme. Each unit has also to drop into its place in the higher formations, and these again must find themselves grouped in position according to the fundamental plan. No change, no alteration is possible during mobilisation. Improvisation when dealing with nearly three million men and the movements of 4,278 trains, as the French had to do, is out of the question.

There were some curious features about these wonderful plans for universal mobilisation. Though they had been worked on and elaborated for many years, they had never been tried in practice. Russia was the only great power which had ever mobilised its great army, and this was for the Russo-Japanese war, not a relevant experience. In that war the Russian armies had to be trickled slowly across the interminable wastes of Siberia, and there could be no question of flinging them all simultaneously into battle. In other countries there were of course manoeuvres and occasional sample tests to see how the time-tables worked. But no one had any idea what would happen when the time really came to mobilise and move men by the million. Some general staffs, especially the German, trusted the efficiency of the railways as well as their own and confidently assumed that no margin need be left for error or misfortune. Others, especially the Russian and the Austrian, expected that things would often go wrong and allowed for this in the time-table.

Right: The British army had won great experience at war: 500,000 British troops were needed to defeat 20,000 Boers. Artillery advancing (top) and bombarding the Boers (bottom)

VAN NE
PHOTO

One interruption was not postulated in any plan for mobilisation: the enemy. It was assumed that, while rates of mobilisation might vary, no power would be allowed a head start on its rivals. But the assumption was carried further, and the plans went on developing with no allowance for enemy interference when weeks might have passed or even when, as in the exceptional German case, the mobilisation was to be completed in some foreign or enemy country. An anecdote from the Crimean war comes to mind. The British Surgeon General, when faced with complaints about the breakdown of the medical services, replied: 'The medical services would have been perfectly adequate if it had not been for the casualties.' Similarly the general staffs could say before 1914: 'Our plans are perfect unless the enemy interferes with them.' Even the manoeuvres which tested the plans to some extent were determined by special moves as in a game. Once a decisive position was occupied, the manoeuvres were over.

Almost total lack of experience
Real fighting was difficult, if not impossible, to simulate, and no staff officers outside Russia had fighting experience of a relevant kind. The Russians had faced problems of logistics during the Russo-Japanese war, but they had learnt little except that war was a chaos. They concluded that the only method was somehow to get the armies together and then to send them lurching forward — a method they applied throughout the First World War. The British army had considerable fighting experience during the Boer War, but this was experience of fast-moving warfare against an elusive enemy, skilled but with small forces. The Italians had got some fighting experience in Abyssinia and Libya, campaigns which did them little credit. The French and Germans had virtually no experience at all. Colonial campaigns in Morocco or against the Hereros of South-West Africa taught few lessons of value. It was peculiarly ironical that Schlieffen, the most influential of all German planners, never took part in any fighting — not even during the Franco-German war, though he was already a serving officer.

These inexperienced strategists all held firmly to the dogma that their plans were immutable to the last detail and that improvisation of any kind was impossible. With each elaboration, they became still more the prisoners of their own time-tables. Mobilisation appeared to them a once-for-all operation. It had to be performed in a particular way and would then determine the entire shape of the war which followed. Moreover, since the plans were prepared and occasionally tested in peacetime, they assumed unconsciously that peacetime conditions would continue after the outbreak of war. The war would be, as

it were, imposed on a peacetime society which would pursue its usual habits. The army trains therefore had to be fitted in not only with each other, but also with the normal traffic in passengers and freight.

Politically the plans for mobilisation were all made in the void. They aimed at the best technical result without allowing for either the political conditions from which war might spring or the political consequences which might follow from any particular plan. There was little consultation between military planners and civilian statesmen. The statesmen assumed that the general staffs were doing their best to ensure that they would win a war if one came, and there was no speculation how policy could be seconded by military action. The dogma of the great Clausewitz that 'war is a continuation of policy by other means' had lost its hold. War had now become a theoretical operation conducted for its own sake. This attitude persisted even when war came. Hence the belligerents fought simply for victory, not to gain any precise, specified advantage.

The military planners were a little more forthcoming towards their allied colleagues, but not to the extent of co-ordinating their plans. The British were the one exception for an obvious reason. Mobilisation within the British Isles would not of itself lead on to war. The army would have to go somewhere outside the country, and the British staff drew up elaborate plans by which it should go to France. In this way, Great Britain, which was supposed from her maritime position to possess the most flexible strategy, acquired the most inflexible. The French made no answering gesture and merely tacked on the British forces to their own. The great French preoccupation lay elsewhere in the fear that, while the Germans were invading France, the Russians would throw all their strength against Austria-Hungary. From the moment when the Franco-Russian alliance was concluded, the French insisted that a considerable proportion of the Russian army should be directed against Germany. **23** ▷

Left: The advocates of peace and the champions of the mailed fist. August Bebel (top left), the leader of the German Social Democratic Party. He talked of a general strike against war without meaning it seriously. Viviani (top right), former socialist and radical orator. French premier in 1914, he led France into war. The elder Moltke (upper centre left), victor in Bismarck's wars, and his nephew (upper centre right), the Kaiser's reluctant warlord. Conrad von Hötzendorf (lower centre left), chief of the Austrian general staff. A much praised strategist who never won a battle. Joseph Caillaux (lower centre right); while he preached peace his wife shot the editor of a leading French newspaper. Berchtold (bottom left); Austro-Hungarian foreign minister, he sought to reassert the Empire's prestige. Grey (bottom right), British foreign minister, who worked to eliminate tension

17825

A great game of make-believe

The great armies never mobilised in peacetime. This would have placed an intolerable strain on the railways, and a general call-up would have disrupted civil life. The general staffs had to spend their time on war games, devising imaginary time-tables of increasing complexity. They were too busy over this to consider what the enemy might be doing. The days of highest pretence came in the summer. Then the generals and their staffs played hard at manoeuvres with elaborate rules which ensured long breaks for meals twice a day. If anyone won the game by an unorthodox move a black mark was set against him. When war came it proved very different from these happy summer festivities with their gay uniforms and bland assumptions. **Left:** A group of German officers in their finery pose for the camera during manoeuvres. **Below:** French soldiers on manoeuvres with a new but little appreciated toy. None of the armies before the First World War appreciated the effect which the machine-gun was to have on the rules by which they played

The Russians willingly produced fanciful figures showing the vast armies available for the German theatre. They were less forthcoming in the practical consideration of building strategic railways to the German frontier. Time and again, the French provided loans to Russia, on condition that part of the money should be spent on such railways. Time and again, the condition was evaded. The Russian time-table, though impressive on paper, thus remained largely a figment of the imagination.

The absence of co-ordination between Germany and Austria-Hungary was even more striking, especially as these were reputed to be 'the military monarchies'. The Germans drew up elaborate plans for moving Italian forces to the French front, and the Italians enjoyed this planning greatly. They did not intend, however, to take part in a war against France and when the time came did not do so. The prolonged discussions were therefore without purpose. Between Germany and Austria-Hungary there was little more than vague talk of making war in common. The Germans suspected that the Austrians might divert all their strength to the Balkans instead of fighting against Russia, but there was little they could do to change this, and they made no attempt to plan a joint campaign against Russia. Certainly the Germans did not rely on the Austrians for the defence of German territory in the east. Instead they relied on time—that is to say, the superior speed of their own mobilisation. They assumed that they would have defeated France before the Russians were prepared to move against East Prussia on any great scale at all.

On a more technical level there was no co-ordination at all. The British and French armies in the west, the German and Austrian armies in the east, would presumably fight side by side. Yet there was no attempt to co-ordinate equipment or intelligence services. No one had thought out a system of liaison between the various allied armies. The Germans had the advantage that they spoke the same language as the Austrians, at any rate at the higher levels of society, but they took few steps to use this advantage in practice. The British and French had made no preparations at all and, when they found themselves fighting side by side, had to rely on any bilingual officer who happened to be available. Even so, when Joffre, the French commander-in-chief, wished to communicate with Sir John French, who commanded the British Expeditionary Force, he usually did so via the British ambassador in Paris.

There were thus half a dozen separate plans for mobilisation, none designed to fit in with any other, except in the British case, and all merging to a greater or lesser

Left: German infantrymen rest during a lull in manoeuvres

extent into plans for actual war. The Russian and Austro-Hungarian plans were the least linked with the war which might actually follow. The Russians merely provided that the armies would gather at their centres of mobilisation. Then the commanders would decide what to do next, whether in fact to attack Austria-Hungary or Germany. Even so, only one type of mobilisation was possible. If the Russians resolved on a limited mobilisation, say of the forces nearest to Austria-Hungary, they could not switch over to a larger mobilisation later. For that would mean that some trains would be running according to the time-table of Day 6 or 10, when others would be running according to the time-table of Day 1. This sort of confusion would be unthinkable.

The Austrians had prepared in theory a more flexible strategy. Even if they operated a general mobilisation, some of the armies were placed in such a position and provided with such alternative time-tables that they could proceed to different fields of battle. The bulk of the army was pointed towards Galicia, where it would encounter the Russians. But three groups could turn against either Serbia or Russia, and two against either Serbia or Italy. The ingenuity with which this was planned gave Conrad, chief of the Austro-Hungarian general staff, the reputation of being the best strategist in Europe. But the ingenuity was mainly on paper. When the time came, the Austrians put off mobilising as long as they could and then improvised in an atmosphere of chaos.

The Russian and Austrian plans had one feature in common: they provided that, after mobilisation, the commanders would look around and decide what to do. In other words, the dogma often heard before the First World War and repeated parrot-like by many historians after it that 'mobilisation means war' did not apply so far as Russia and Austria-Hungary were concerned. For them mobilisation meant mobilisation: greater readiness to fight a war, but not a final decision to fight it, and still less a decision where and how it would be fought. The distinction between mobilisation and war was less clear on the western front.

The French had no doubt where their war would be fought. Indeed they were the one country for whom any choice of strategy was inconceivable. Their only possible war was against Germany, and the only possible place for the French to fight it was on the short Franco-German frontier of the Vosges. The French plans were designed to ensure that all their armies would be in a position to fight this great battle of the frontiers as soon as possible after the beginning of mobilisation. For many years, the French had planned a purely defensive battle—to keep the Germans out of France. Latterly their commanders had come

to believe that a defensive strategy was bound to fail and that an offensive one was bound to succeed. They therefore proposed to rush bull-headed against the Germans.

There was a further reason for this change of strategy. The French suspected that the Germans might try to turn their northern flank by going through Belgium. The French could not plan to violate Belgian neutrality first, if only for fear of offending British feeling, and any move into Belgium after the Germans had entered it would be that impossible thing—improvisation. However, the French were undismayed. They thought that they knew the answer. Since they refused to believe that the Germans could use reservists as front-line soldiers, they greatly underestimated the forces at Germany's disposal and assumed that the Germans could send armies into Belgium only by weakening their centre. Hence a victory for the French offensive was even more certain.

Birth of the Schlieffen plan

French mobilisation was very near to war, but not quite war. Once the French armies were assembled on the frontier, they could wait for the signal to attack. Indeed they had to wait until they knew whether the Germans were going through Belgium or not. This news would determine both the weight and the place of their own attack. With the Germans, and only with the Germans, there was no breathing space between mobilisation and war. One merged inevitably into the other, and this proved the decisive impulse towards war in August 1914. This unique feature of German planning had been developing for a generation past. It sprang from Germany's unique position. Alone among the great powers she had two potentially hostile great powers, France and Russia, as neighbours and would have to fight two great wars with one army. The elder Moltke, victor of the Franco-German war, had proposed to hold the narrow French frontier with its strong fortifications, while the bulk of the German army defeated the Russian. His successor, Schlieffen, rejected this strategy. Like everyone else, he doubted whether a defensive could succeed. In any case, the defeat of Russia would not be decisive. Great Russian armies would remain somewhere in Russia's vast space, and the Germans would be entangled in a prolonged campaign, while the French broke through in the west.

Schlieffen therefore proposed to fight the western battle first. France would be defeated, Paris would be taken, and the Germans could then turn all their strength against Russia. Originally, when Schlieffen switched the weight

Left: The fancier the dress, the more certain the victory. Austrian officers at their most gorgeously incompetent

of German attack from east to west, he thought only of a battle of the frontiers, just as the French did. Soon he decided that the French line of fortresses was too strong to be broken in a hurry, and, with Russian armies massing in the east, the Germans would have no time to spare. The French line would therefore have to be outflanked on either south or north. A southern flanking movement through Switzerland would not put the Germans across the French lines of communication, nor would it lead to any centres of French strength. Schlieffen therefore rejected it. A northern advance through Luxembourg and Belgium offered greater rewards. The German armies would move through easy country. They would soon be in a position to encircle the French armies and to threaten Paris, or so Schlieffen imagined (see page 115).

Schlieffen was a professor of strategy, not a practical general. He played with his plan for many years, making it ever more elaborate. At first he intended to go only through Luxembourg and a corner of Belgium. Later he became more ambitious and proposed to sweep right through Belgium into northern France. Ultimately he allotted four armies, two-thirds of Germany's strength in the west, for this great stroke. There was only a narrow gap of 80 miles between the supposedly impassable Ardennes and the frontier of Holland, which the Germans proposed to respect. The four armies must pass through Aachen, the only railway junction, and then be pumped through this narrow gap before the French realised what was happening. It was impossible for all four armies to mobilise at Aachen and then wait for the declaration of war. The first army must mobilise and be on its way before the second arrived, and so on. Schlieffen therefore included the invasion of Belgium in his plans for mobilisation. More correctly, he had no plans for mobilisation. Once the Germans began to mobilise, war inevitably followed on the second or third day, unless of course the Belgians gave the German armies a free run.

Schlieffen never worried about the political problem of Belgian neutrality. He did not speculate as to whether the Belgians would resist. He did not reflect that the infringement of Belgian neutrality might bring Great Britain into a war against Germany—a consideration which, in view of the small size of the British army, did not interest him. His anxieties were purely technical. For instance, the Belgians had a great fortress, Liège, immediately barring the way against the Germans. This, far from making Schlieffen hesitate, determined him to act even more at a rush and to take Liège almost before the Belgians knew what was happening. Again, in his re-

Right: The launching of another battleship for the German fleet

morselessly academic way, he pushed on to consider remote contingencies, which might arise on the twentieth
or even the fortieth day. He would need one army to seal
off Antwerp, another to guard the German lines of communication, and still more fresh armies when the Germans arrived in front of Paris. The only contingency he
never considered was that the French might at some time
realise what was happening and get in his way. The entire
Schlieffen plan was conceived as a peacetime manoeuvre.
In the end, he decided that he could not provide enough
forces for a decisive victory. His plan was 'an enterprise
beyond our strength', and his only practical conclusion
was that the government must raise larger forces.

Still, the Schlieffen plan was all the Germans had.
When Schlieffen retired, he was succeeded by Moltke's
nephew, and this younger Moltke, a courtier not a strategist, simply relied on the drafts which he found in Schlieffen's drawer. The marshalling yards at Aachen were increased still more. The time-tables went on being elaborated. The German general staff did not tell the civilian
statesmen what was being prepared, and the statesmen
tactfully did not ask. It was not, they thought, their affair.
They conducted German policy or tried to. If war came,
the generals would win it, and there was no overlap between one task and the other.

After this grandiose plan, which envisaged the greatest
battle in history, British intentions seem on a small scale.
Yet they too were to have immense consequences. Until
after the Boer War, the British had no army for continental purposes. Their armed forces existed only for
colonial warfare and for the defence of India. In the first
decade of the 20th century, the British built up an expeditionary force of three army corps for use on the continent
of Europe. Their original intention, so far as it existed,
was to send this force on some kind of independent venture, sustained by British sea power. Mobilisation would
be completed in England, and any decision what to do
with the expeditionary force would be made later. As
time went by, the French began to press for a promise of
British support. The British would not give this promise,
but they saw no harm in answering that they could
actually provide the support if they decided to do so. There
were staff conversations with the French, which worked
out a time-table for the BEF to arrive on the left of the
French line. The civilian statesmen insisted that there
was no firm promise involved in these conversations, and
their insistence was accepted. The statesmen did not realise that, in a sense, they were committed all the same.

**European
diplomacy, 1914**
Entente powers, 1914
Allies and associates of
the Entente powers
Neutral states, 1914
Central powers, 1914
Neutral states on
outbreak of war
which later allied
with the Entente powers

**Major
European
railways, 1914**

Top right: The political tangle, the system of rival alliances
Bottom right: A tangle of lines, the intricate railway network

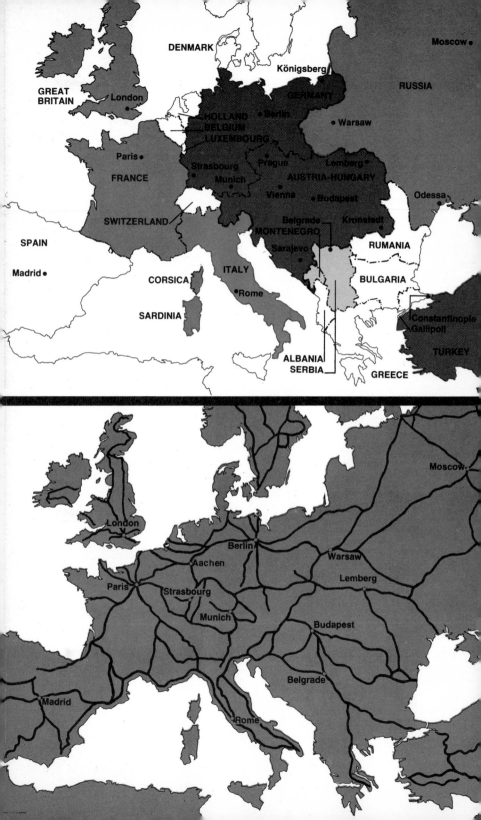

They could decide whether or not to go to war. But if they decided for war, then the plans established with the French were the only ones which could operate. Once at war, the BEF must go to Maubeuge in north-eastern France and nowhere else in the wide expanses of Europe.

Every great power also possessed a navy of some size, and there were plans for naval mobilisation. Here, with one exception, the time-tables stopped. The fleets would assemble in their bases and then, for the most part, conduct a defensive strategy, mainly protecting the coasts from invasion and coastal shipping from interference. None of the navies except one had any offensive intention. Their purpose was to ward off the enemy ships rather than to challenge and join combat with them. The one exception was Great Britain. Certainly the Royal Navy had many cruisers and smaller ships for policing trade routes all over the world. But its pride was the Grand Fleet, the greatest assembly of the most powerful ships ever known. On mobilisation, the Grand Fleet would proceed to its wartime base at Scapa Flow. Shortly afterwards, according to Admiral Lord Fisher, its principal creator, it would sally forth into the North Sea and would there destroy the German fleet at a true Armageddon. This plan was in curious contrast with most army ones, which were assumed to operate without any interference by the enemy. Fisher's plan was the exact opposite. It assumed that the enemy fleet would conveniently attend on its destruction, whenever it suited the Royal Navy.

This assumption was unfounded. The Germans, too, had a battle fleet on which they had lavished much money and for the sake of which they had jeopardised their relations with Great Britain. But they had no plan for using it in wartime. The German fleet was supposed to present the Royal Navy with some vague menace and thus to secure British neutrality, if not friendship. Once war broke out, it would have failed in its purpose, and it must be kept safe until some other possibility of menace was restored. The only German naval plan was therefore that the fleet should remain in harbour. Yet the Germans could have caused great damage to the British if they had forgotten about the British Grand Fleet away at Scapa Flow. They could for instance have raided the British sea communications with France and been safely back in harbour before the British Grand Fleet could come south. But the Germans never thought of it. They were as convinced as the British that the one purpose of a battle fleet was to engage another and, in a sense, they defeated the entire purpose of the British simply by keeping out of the way.

Left: The greatest fleet in the world displays its might; the Grand Fleet dressed overall for the coronation review in 1910

31

To judge solely from the military and naval plans, all the great powers were in imminent peril and on the brink of war. It seems astonishing that the generals and admirals had not pulled the lever long before. In truth, their plans had become a habit. Few of these great warriors had ever heard a shot fired in anger, and they hardly connected this experience with their plans. On the surface at least, all the plans were defensive. All, even that of the Germans, were designed to win a war if one happened, not to bring one about. Though many generals and some admirals talked of war as desirable in order to clear the air or to improve the national character, none of them tried to turn their talk into action. They waited for the civilian statesmen to give the warning that the country was in danger, when no doubt they would save it. The statesmen, not the commanders, brought on the outbreak of war in 1914.

A general easing of tension

Yet few, if any, of the statesmen were more eager for war than they had been earlier. They all wanted their particular country to be secure and even to triumph in diplomatic encounters. But they had not changed their patterns of general behaviour which had somehow kept Europe at peace for more than thirty years past. The particular statesmen who happened to be in power in 1914 were not markedly more incompetent than their predecessors and certainly not more bellicose. The international situation was no more tense in the summer of 1914 than it had been previously, indeed in many ways a good deal less so. European relations had changed with remarkable rapidity in the previous few years. The alliances, though still rigid in theory, appeared much less so in practice. Almost every power played with the idea of changing its partners. The atmosphere of reshuffle began in 1911. In that year the French set out to establish a protectorate over Morocco. The Germans claimed compensation for the rights which they possessed under the agreement of Algeciras, made in 1906. Caillaux, the French premier, was willing to pay the German price. He knew that he could expect no support from his nominal ally, Russia. In any case, he hoped to escape by a reconciliation between France and Germany. The protests came from Great Britain. British statesmen were afraid that France would appease Germany by concessions at their expense. British statesmen, not French, turned the confrontation into a war crisis. The British fleet was mobilised, not the French or German armies. In the end, Germany and France reached agreement despite British protests.

This crisis had curious results. French opinion was

offended by the agreement with Germany; British opinion was offended by the nearness of armed conflict. In France, there was a revival of national spirit, more assertively patriotic than at any time since the establishment of the Third Republic. French statesmen put aside the reserve with which they had previously treated their Russian ally. Now the Russians were told that they could count on French support, however the conflict happened to start. There was of course an implicit moral that the Russians should make the same assurances the other way round.

The British on the other hand laboured to redress the grievances from which Germany was supposed to be suffering. Reconciliation with Germany was pursued as steadfastly as reconciliation with France and Russia had been pursued earlier. The British laid aside their own grievance against the German challenge of naval rivalry and accepted the German navy as a given fact of the international scene. The Germans claimed to be short of colonies, and the British earnestly pressed the Portuguese colonies upon them — not forgetting of course to take a cut for themselves. The Germans also wanted British approval for the railway which they were building across Asia Minor, ultimately to Baghdad. The British dropped their old objections, again after securing their own interests. These were somewhat sordid transactions, buying Anglo-German friendship at the expense of other people. But the purchase was successful. Great Britain and Germany moved on to closer terms than for ten or fifteen years past.

The first European war of the 20th century broke out in the autumn of 1912, when all the Balkan states except Rumania attacked the Ottoman or Turkish Empire and carried off most of Turkey-in-Europe. This war was both a humiliation and a success for the Concert of Europe. On the one hand, small powers defied great ones. The great powers forbade the Balkan states to attack Turkey and warned them that if they did so they would not be allowed to acquire any Turkish territory. The Balkan states took no notice, went to war, and annexed Turkish territory without any attempt being made to stop them. On the other hand, the great powers remained at peace among themselves. For years past diplomats had been saying that a great European war would break out 'when the snow melted on the Balkan mountains'. The snow melted metaphorically, yet no great war followed. **39** ▷

Left: *Prisoners taken during the Balkan Wars. These, the first European wars of the 20th century, were a misleading prelude to the First World War. The soldiers had very few machine-guns and relied mainly on the bayonet. It seemed that decisive victories would still be won by mass and manoeuvre. Only at the end did the Turks recover by belatedly digging trenches*

Storm and stress in civilian life

Disturbances in art and politics seemed to foreshadow the disturbances of war. It was as though men and women sensed the coming of war and contributed their individual mite of destruction before war destroyed them all. The new music shattered accepted harmonies, women demanded the vote and abandoned their feminine modesty, working men demanded higher wages and threatened a general strike which would bring capitalism to an end. **Far right:** Nijinsky, famous for his leap. When Stravinsky's ballet *Le Sacre du Printemps (The Rite of Spring)* was first performed in Paris, rioters repeatedly wrecked the theatre until the performances were abandoned. **Right:** English suffragettes set an example which women followed in other countries. Here a French suffragette is being arrested by the police. **Below:** Some suffragettes preached socialism as well. Here a former suffragette has been transformed into a strike leader. **Next page:** 'The Farewells' by Umberto Boccioni, a Futurist premonition of the war which was hanging over Europe.

The great powers kept in touch by means of a conference of ambassadors which met regularly under Grey's chairmanship in London. The two powers most closely concerned with the Balkans, Russia and Austria-Hungary, laid down their irreducible minimum. Russia would not tolerate the Bulgarians in Constantinople; Austria-Hungary would not tolerate the Serbs on the Adriatic. Both conditions were met, partly by the accidents of war, partly by demonstrations of force on the part of the great powers. The nationalities of the Balkans were liberated. The great Balkan question which had racked international relations for a couple of centuries seemed to have been solved without provoking a general disturbance.

A few remaining problems
Of course there were still problems left over. The Ottoman Empire seemed on the point of disintegration, and the Russians were bound to worry about the future of Constantinople and the Straits. The victory of nationalism in the Balkans provoked a stir among the subject nationalities of Austria-Hungary, especially among the Serbs. But these were problems for the future. The Turks were still alive and in fact recovering some of their military strength now that they had lost most of Turkey-in-Europe. The Serbs were exhausted by the Balkan war and in no position to face a new war against Austria-Hungary. The greatest fear which had haunted Europe—a war between Russia and Austria-Hungary—seemed to have been removed. The so-called prizes of the Balkans were no longer there for them to fight over. The Balkan states had taken the prizes for themselves.

Historians, enjoying the advantage of hindsight, have discovered all sorts of indications in the spring of 1914 that a great European war was about to break out. The great powers were spending more on armaments than ever before, though economists of a more sophisticated age might have pointed out that in these boom years the powers were not spending on armaments a greater proportion of their national income. Violence was in the air—strikes in Russia, suffragettes in England, chaos in the Austrian parliament, Futurists in Italy. Even the ethereal world of the ballet was disturbed, and riots broke out in Paris whenever *Le Sacre du Printemps* was performed. Yet was this violence new or unusual? Wagner's music had once provoked as many riots as ever Stravinsky's did.

Top left: As the Agadir crisis of 1911 smoulders, France and Spain appeal to 'Uncle Bull' to stop the German baby playing in the Moroccan pond. **Bottom left:** *The mailed fist of the Kaiser.* **Near left:** *Delegates arrive for the conference at Algeciras in 1906 which failed to settle the Morocco question*

The Austrian parliament had seen worse chaos seventeen years before. The suffragettes were less destructive than the Fenians. For the ordinary person, Europe was more peaceful than it had ever been before or was to be afterwards. For the only time in history, the private citizen could wander almost anywhere across Europe without check from the police or danger from brigands. Again for the only time in history, the private citizen could count on a reasonably free trial almost anywhere in Europe even for a political offence.

Contemporary observers, who did not know what was going to happen, often guessed in an exactly contrary way. It looked as though the system of alliances was breaking up. Now that the Balkan question was settled, there seemed little reason why Germany should need to back Austria-Hungary, or why France, and still less Great Britain, should back Russia any more. French financiers were reconciled with German, and Franco-German heavy industry was as much a combine as it became later in the Common Market. Great Britain and Germany were each other's best customers. The three advanced industrial countries of western Europe were drawing together for a co-operative exploitation of the rest of the world. Enlightened Frenchmen were glad to be rid of Russia. Even German diplomats believed that the Austrian alliance was an encumbrance which should be shaken off.

There still seemed plenty of room in the world for the imperialist powers. Germany had plans for building an empire in central Africa from one ocean to another, and there was no objection except from the helpless Belgians — many even of whom would be glad to give up the Congo. Turkey-in-Asia was ripe for partition into economic spheres of influence, and only Russia would object if the remnants of the Ottoman Empire were at last modernised. China offered a still larger field for imperialist partnership, with Germany and the United States already co-operating against the two reactionary powers, Japan and Russia, while Great Britain tardily moved towards the side of progress. Industrial and financial interests were everywhere pulling the rich together against the poor and backward, and economic factors which have been blamed for the First World War were in fact the greatest security of peace. The capitalists of every country cried against war in the crisis of July 1914. Capitalism did not rule the world in any political sense. This negative fact ranks high among the causes of the First World War.

The people were supposed to rule. There was universal suffrage in France, Germany, Italy (only since 1912), and Austria, though not in Hungary. There was household suffrage in the United Kingdom. There was suffrage of a sort even in Russia, though the Duma had few powers.

There had certainly been times when the people had responded to the call of imperialism and even of war. The British people had been eager to go to war with France during the Fashoda crisis of 1898 and had exploded into jingoism during the Boer War. The French people had resented the compromise with Germany after the Agadir affair. The German people had resented the same crisis even more sharply.

'A springtime of radical confidence'
By 1914 the tide was running the other way. Jingoism and imperial rhetoric were no longer winning cries at the polls. The Social Democrats were the largest single party in the German Reichstag, and they were pledged in theory to an attitude of war resistance. In France a general election of April 1914 produced a majority of Radicals and Socialists who repudiated the previous policy of militarism and aggressive alliance with Russia. Caillaux, the Radical leader, was an advocate of co-operation with Germany. Jaurès, the Socialist leader, was the greatest advocate in Europe of conciliation and international friendship. President Poincaré, champion of revenge, gloomily faced the prospect of having to appoint a pro-German pacific prime minister. A stroke of luck, bad or good, saved him from the worst. Caillaux's second wife, pursued with libellous hostility by his first, shot dead the editor of a Paris newspaper. The scandal ruled out Caillaux as prime minister. Viviani, the substitute, was less clear-headed and less competent. Poincaré could count for something after all.

Tory imperialism was on the run in the United Kingdom. British army-officers in Ireland, prodded on by the Unionist Party, had staged a near-mutiny rather than coerce the Protestants of Ulster. The resultant outcry made the Tories for once the unpatriotic party. Liberals and Labour drew together in a common programme of peace and social reform. Lloyd George, Chancellor of the Exchequer, announced confidently that hostility between Germany and Great Britain was at an end, and this announcement seemed likely to be a winning card at the next election. This was a springtime of radical confidence. It is tempting to suggest that the old ruling classes of Europe launched a great war in the realisation that otherwise power would slip from their grasp. But this would credit them with too much intelligence and directive ability. The old gang had little idea what they were doing and drifted haphazardly from one problem to the next. Though their prestige was declining, their wealth was increasing, and this was no situation for dangerous

Left: A German Hussar and his wife parade together in uniform

courses. Few people believed that war would provoke general revolution. On the other hand, even fewer believed that war would prevent revolution. The balance between the factors maintaining peace and those pulling towards war seemed no different in 1914 than it had been throughout the previous generation, and war therefore was no more likely to occur than it had been previously.

The deeper problem of Germany

There was perhaps one difference in 1914, a difference of emphasis rather than of nature. In nearly all European countries the forces making for war were much what they had always been — silly old generals who had never seen fighting, pedantic diplomats who had been told by someone or other that they should guard the national honour, hack journalists who could pull in an odd penny by writing a jingoistic piece. These were diseases of an endemic nature present in every modern society and did no harm except to themselves. In Germany militarism went deeper. Here was the only society where army officers determined the moral tone of public life as well as of their own military circle. University professors and bank directors took pride in their rank as army reservists, a quirk rarely encountered in England or France. Military values determined the tone of German policy in a way that was not true elsewhere. Of course Russia too would have been a 'military monarchy', if it had been capable of being anything. But in the general deliquescence of the tsarist regime, the Russian system had ceased to have any character.

Germany had displayed a peculiarly militaristic character ever since the foundation of the second Reich in 1871. Generals had always set the social tone, and the constitution had always been twisted in favour of the army. But in earlier years, particularly during Bismarck's time, the army and its leaders had existed for defensive purposes. Bismarck had certainly taught that Germany would perish unless she were the most militaristic of the great powers, but that was all he had taught. Indeed, in Bismarck's view, Germany had to be militaristic because she was weak. Since then Germany had grown increasingly strong. Few Germans doubted that their country was the greatest of European powers. From this it was an easy step to feeling that she was receiving less than her due. Germans were aggrieved that

*Right: Some of the problems which beset the great powers on the eve of war. The Kaiser finds that the many-headed monster of Social Democracy refuses to die (**bottom right**). Political scandal in France, Madame Caillaux shoots the editor of* Le Figaro *(**top right**). Ulster volunteers in training (**near right**); their defiance brought Great Britain to the brink of civil war*

		Great Britain	France	Russia	Turkey
	Population	46,407,037	39,601,509	167,000,000	21,373,900
	Soldiers available on mobilisation	711,000[1]	3,500,000	4,423,000[2]	360,000
	Merchant fleet (net steam tonnage)	11,538,000	1,098,000	(1913) 486,914	(1911) 66,878
	Battleships (built and being built)	64	28	16	
	Cruisers	121	34	14	
	Submarines	64	73	29	
	Annual value of foreign trade (£)	1,223,152,000	424,000,000	190,247,000	67,472,000
	Annual steel production (tons)	6,903,000	4,333,000	4,416,000	
	Railway mileage	23,441	25,471	46,573	3,882

[1] including Empire   [2] immediate mobilisation   [3] emergency maximum

they had come late to the distribution of colonies. Hence their demand for 'a place in the sun'. This was comparatively harmless. There were plenty of sunny places still waiting to be allotted, and Germany could have had them. But many Germans slipped into the habit of believing that Germany should exercise a sort of general control over Europe, as France had done or was supposed to have done in the reign of Louis XIV and had certainly done during the Napoleonic Empire. Berlin should succeed Paris as the political, and London as the economic, capital of Europe. When this did not happen, Germans came near to thinking that German power should be used to exact the tribute which others refused to pay voluntarily. Assertiveness, though not perhaps open aggressiveness, had become a predominant German characteristic before 1914. When this was added to the traditional respect which Germans accorded to their military chiefs, Germany became the most dangerous power in Europe.

Comparatively few Germans had conscious plans for a German domination of Europe, and still fewer tried to give such plans practical shape. Most Germans in positions of high authority did not appreciate how far they had drifted from the general European outlook. They were aggrieved and bewildered when others rejected the proffered hand which they supposed they were holding out. In their view, they would be delighted to protect the British Empire as they had long protected the Austrian Empire; delighted to patronise France as they patronised Italy; delighted, most of all, to assist the Russian tsar against his revolutionary subjects. It was strange and exasperating when others did not share this view. They inclined more and more to rely on Germany's 'sharp sword' – the sort of out-of-date military phrase used by public men in every country. All imagined a war of glamour and heroics, with swords and cavalry charges. They got something quite different.

It is the fashion nowadays to seek profound causes for great events. But perhaps the war which broke out in 1914 had no profound causes. For thirty years past, international diplomacy, the balance of power, the alliances, and the accumulation of armed might produced peace. Suddenly the situation was turned round, and the very forces which had produced the long peace now produced a great war. In much the same way, a motorist who for thirty years has been doing the right thing to avoid accidents makes a mistake one day and has a crash. In July 1914 things went wrong. The only safe explanation in history is that things happen because they happen.

ermany	Austria-Hungary
,000,000	49,882,231
500,000¹	3,000,000
096,000	(1912) 559,784
)	16
	12
	6
030,380,000	198,712,000
,024,000	2,642,000
,439	27,545

Left: The real balance of power in Europe with Germany economically and militarily moving well ahead of all her potential rivals

45

Chapter 2
Meeting at Sarajevo

The occasion for the First World War was provided by two shots fired at Sarajevo, capital of Bosnia, on 28th June 1914. With these shots Gavrilo Princip, a Bosnian student, killed Archduke Franz Ferdinand and his morganatic wife Sophie, Duchess of Hohenberg. The Archduke and the student were symbolic figures. Franz Ferdinand was the nephew and presumptive heir of Franz Joseph, Emperor of Austria, Apostolic King of Hungary, King, Archduke, Grand Duke, Count, and Lord of this, that and the other – to say nothing of being titular King of Jerusalem. The Archduke was also Inspector General of the Austro-Hungarian army. He personified the Habsburg monarchy, which had ranked high among the great powers of Europe for almost five hundred years. Throughout that time, though rarely successful in wars, it had somehow survived. It had championed Christendom against the Turks and the Counter-Reformation against the Protestants. It had resisted the French Revolution and the great Napoleon. Now, with its conglomeration of eleven different nationalities (or, with the Jews, twelve), it seemed to represent historic right against national freedom. In practice, this worked out as German and Magyar, or Hungarian, domination over the rest. Franz Ferdinand, an absolutist by nature, disliked the two dominant nationalities as much as he disliked the other peoples over whom he was destined never to rule.

The student was the son of a Bosnian farmer. When Bosnia was under the Turks, some of his ancestors had been Turkish gendarmes. His grandfather had taken part in the rebellion of 1875 against them. Princip followed in his grandfather's footsteps. Though a Bosnian subject, he was a Serb by nationality and sentiment. When he first crossed the border into Serbia, he fell on his knees and kissed the national soil. In 1912, when Serbia launched a war of liberation against Turkey, Princip tried to enlist as a Serb guerilla. He was rejected as too young and too puny. Now he had just finished at secondary school.

Left: A photograph said to be of the arrest of Princip a few seconds after the assassination of Archduke Franz Ferdinand

He ranked as a student in the sense that he had left school and not started on any career. He wanted to do something great for the cause of national liberation. Not, however, for the Serbs alone. Like other young idealists, Princip hoped for a union of all the South Slavs. His nationalism was only part of his revolutionary spirit. He was half-anarchist, half-socialist. He and his friends claimed to belong to *Young Bosnia,* an echo of Mazzini's *Young Italy* in the previous century. They were close in spirit to the Irish enthusiasts who made the Easter rising in 1916. Vladimir Dedijer, the modern Yugoslav historian who understands Princip and his friends best, calls them 'primitive rebels'. Perhaps they were not so primitive. Twenty years later they would have fought in the Spanish civil war. Today they would be at home among the rebellious students who have recently caused a general European turmoil. Princip was in fact the eternal student with the particular grievance that his nation was denied national freedom under the Habsburg yoke.

The fatal meeting is arranged

The encounter between the Archduke and the student had been fixed for some time, at least since the previous March, when it had been decided to hold the principal summer manoeuvres of the Austro-Hungarian army in Bosnia and the Archduke had decided to attend them. This was an obvious political gesture. The Serbs under Turkish rule had been liberated by the Balkan wars of 1912 and 1913. Talk of liberating the Serbs or even the South Slavs under Habsburg rule naturally followed, though more in Bosnia than in Serbia, which had been exhausted by the previous war. The Austro-Hungarian government had declared that it would not tolerate any acquisition of Turkish territory by Serbia. When this happened all the same, Austria-Hungary had done little except to limit Serb claims against Albania. The Habsburgs seemed to be losing in their stand against nationalism. The moment for defiance had come. The Austro-Hungarian army would demonstrate its might in Bosnia, and the heir to the throne himself would add political weight to the demonstration.

It is tempting to suggest that the date for the fatal meeting had been fixed further back in history. 28th June was the day of St Vitus, patron saint of Serbia. On that day in 1389 the last army of old Serbia had been

Left: The traditional glory of the oldest dynasty in Europe was challenged by the nationalistic aspirations of a people who had barely left the Middle Ages. The Habsburgs seemed invincible in their imperial finery (top) but their empire was to be destroyed by the humble people of Serbia (bottom) who had only gained independence in 1878 after a war against the Turks

destroyed by the Ottoman Turks at the battle of Kosovo Field. Revenge came only in the autumn of 1912 when the army of new Serbia defeated the Turks at the battle of Kumanovo. It would have been strikingly appropriate if the Archduke had defied Serb feeling by visiting Sarajevo on their sacred national day. There is no evidence that the connection was made. The Habsburgs knew nothing of the national traditions of the peoples over whom they ruled. Probably the Archduke and his advisers had never heard of Kosovo. At most, they were vaguely aware that 28th June was some sort of holiday in Bosnia and therefore suitable for a ceremonial visit.

Two significant coincidences

28th June had, however, another significance. In 1900 the Archduke married on that day. His bride, Sophie Chotek, belonged to an old and aristocratic Bohemian family, but she did not come within the 'permitted degrees', suitable for a member of the Habsburg house. She was merely aristocratic, not royal or imperial, and therefore was not allowed to share her husband's rank. Their children were disinherited. At court ceremonies, she had to follow the youngest archduchess. Franz Ferdinand bitterly resented these humiliations to his wife. If he came to Bosnia, it would be as Inspector General and Field-Marshal, not as Archduke. It would be a purely military occasion, and his wife would ride by his side. There could be no better celebration for their wedding anniversary. Once more, there is no evidence that the connection was made. Perhaps the coincidence with the Archduke's wedding-day, like that with the day of Kosovo, was an accident, which no one noticed at the time. The Archduke had simply decided to defy Serb feeling, and his wife loyally went with him.

Princip was in Belgrade, waiting for the results of his final examination, when a Bosnian friend sent him a cutting from a Sarajevo newspaper. It contained the announcement of the Archduke's coming visit. This was a great moment for Princip. He had long wished to strike a blow for national freedom, if not by fighting in war, then by assassinating somebody. He had talked of assassinating General Potiorek, the governor of Bosnia. Franz Ferdinand was an even more attractive target. 54 ▷

Near right: The shot which fired the train for the world war. Archduke Franz Ferdinand and his wife leave Sarajevo town hall on their last journey. Top right: The target, Archduke Franz Ferdinand, heir of Franz Joseph, ruler of the Habsburg monarchy. Bottom right: A glamorised impression of the assassination as it might have been. Next page: The aged Emperor Franz Joseph and his court, he stands facing the Archduke Franz Ferdinand—tawdry glitter sustained a decaying Empire

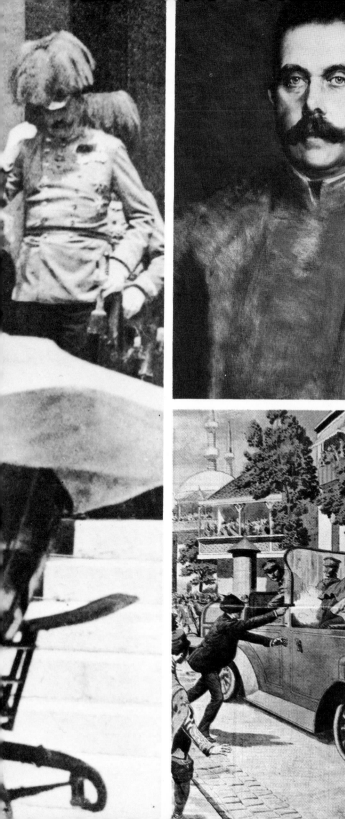

Contrary to the common belief, Princip was not a member of any secret society, except those he invented with other Bosnian schoolboys. But he had a contact, though he probably did not know it, with one such secret nationalist society, the Black Hand.

An intricate and tangled web

This had been originally an association of Serb officers, who had something to do with the assassination of King Alexander Obrenović in 1903. After this, it ran guerillas into Macedonia, not so much to injure the Turks as to compete with the Bulgarians who also claimed Macedonia. This activity gave out in 1913, when Macedonia was liberated and most of it seized, in defiance of Bulgaria, by Serbia. Now the Black Hand was in conflict with the Serbian government. It wanted army officers to control Macedonia, whereas the government determined to establish civilian rule. The conflict was the odder in that 'Apis', head of the Black Hand, was in real life Colonel Dimitrijević, head of the Serbian military intelligence. Apis managed to engineer the dismissal of his enemy Pašić, the prime minister. Then things went wrong. King Peter, who had backed Apis, wearied of public life and handed over power to Crown Prince Alexander, who hated Apis. At the same time, Hartvig, the Russian minister in Belgrade, who had previously backed Apis also, announced that Russia wanted no new troubles in the Balkans. Pašić returned to power and determined on a general election, which would silence the Black Hand for good.

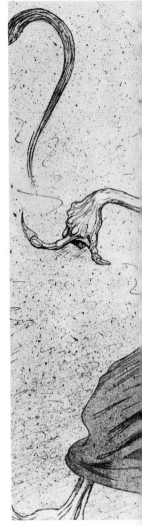

In such circumstances, the thoughts of Apis were directed towards Pašić, not towards the remote Habsburg Archduke. All the speculations that Apis arranged the assassination of the Archduke as the man who might conciliate the South Slavs when he came to the throne and so thwart plans for a great Yugoslavia are so much poppycock, if only because Apis cared solely for the Serbs, not for the South Slavs. Here again, it is tempting to suggest that Apis wanted to make trouble for Pašić. If there was an attempt at assassination in Sarajevo, the Austrians would protest to Belgrade, particularly if they knew that the assassins had come from there. If Pašić gave way, he would be discredited in Serb eyes; if he defied Austria-Hungary, he would again need the support of the nationalist Black Hand. Unfortunately there is no evidence that Apis knew of the plans to assassinate Franz Ferdinand until they were well launched. The connection between Princip and the Black Hand was yet another accident.

Princip himself never knew that he had been in contact with the Black Hand. He only knew that in 1912, when he had tried to enlist, he had been directed to a Major Tankosić, who turned him down. Now he went to Tankosić

again, as the only Serb he knew, and so stumbled on the right person. For Tankosić, as the organiser of guerillas, kept the stock of weapons, with which these guerillas were equipped for Macedonia. Now, though he had no use for them, he had a few left. He agreed to let Princip have half a dozen bombs and revolvers. Later he said that he did this 'to embarrass Pašić'. It is more likely that, having worked himself out of a job in Macedonia, he was glad to stir up trouble in Bosnia. In any case, handing out weapons was a routine operation for Tankosić, and it did not occur to him to consult Apis or any other member of the Black Hand.

Princip enlisted two other Bosnian students with whom he went around in Belgrade. He also wrote to a slightly older friend called Ilić in Sarajevo that they needed three more, whom Ilić duly found. In this way Ilić became the organiser of the affair. It is possible that he really was a member of the Black Hand, though the only evidence for this was provided by Ilić himself when he was trying to save his neck. But his instructions came only from Princip. Tankosić gave the three conspirators further assistance by helping to smuggle them across the Bosnian frontier with their weapons—again a routine operation like the old Macedonian days. The three young men talked indiscreetly about their mission, to the subsequent ruin of those who sheltered them.

No news of the crossing reached the Austrian authorities. The police and the civil officials were in any case not trying very hard. They thought that the Archduke's visit was a risky project and would have advised against it if they had been consulted. But they were not. The visit was laid on as a purely military affair, and the army authorities were confident there would be no trouble. The civil officials were therefore sulking. They took no precautions. When Franz Joseph visited Sarajevo in 1910, hundreds of political suspects were imprisoned for the day and thousands of extra police were brought in. Now no one was arrested, and 120 police provided the only security in a town of 50,000 inhabitants. The military held that it was unnecessary to line the Archduke's route with soldiers. He was to travel unprotected except by Habsburg prestige.

The Serbian government learnt that some men with arms had crossed the Bosnian frontier. It had its agents in the Black Hand and called Apis to order. He, in his

Left: Two men who were allegedly behind the assassination at Sarajevo but who were really in combat with each other. Colonel Dimitrijević, Apis, head of the Black Hand (top left), and Pašić, prime minister of Serbia (top right). Death poses the question: 'Unhappy Austria, what do you do now?' (bottom), a question which Europe wondered for four weeks while Austria-Hungary laboriously tried to think of a demand to make of Serbia

turn, learnt from Tankosić what had happened. The committee of the Black Hand resolved that the attempt on the Archduke must be stopped. Apis sent an agent into Bosnia, and this agent summoned Ilić, the only contact he had. Ilić was told that the attempt must not take place. He returned to Sarajevo and told Princip, who, not being a member of the Black Hand, took no notice. Ilić reluctantly went on with his friends. It is possible that Apis was two-timing. On the day of the assassination, another of his agents appeared in Sarajevo and may have told the conspirators to go ahead. The point has little significance one way or the other. Princip and his friends made their own decisions and did not take orders from the Black Hand.

The Serbian government also attempted to give a warning in Vienna. This was a tricky business. The Serbian government did not know the names of the conspirators and in any case could not actually betray Serb patriots. The Serbian minister in Vienna had therefore to fall back on vague hints of trouble. A Serb soldier in the Austro-Hungarian army, for instance, might load his rifle with live ammunition and kill the Archduke by mistake. Naturally such hints only gave offence. Moreover, the Serbian minister got on to the wrong man — not that there was a right one. He spoke to Biliński, the Austro-Hungarian minister of finance. Biliński was certainly in charge of Bosnia, for want of anything better to do. But he was merely head of the civil administration and had no authority over the army. Also he was on bad terms with Franz Ferdinand. Biliński therefore did not pass on the warning, though again it would have made no difference if he had. Any threat of danger at Sarajevo would have made the Archduke even more determined to go.

The Archduke arrives on time
So the stage was set. On 25th June Franz Ferdinand and his wife arrived at Ilidže, a spa outside Sarajevo, which served as military headquarters. The Archduke inspected troops and attended manoeuvres. He and his wife drove informally into Sarajevo, where they visited the ethnographical museum and had a drink at the principal hotel. They were received with cheers. Everything augured well for the ceremonial visit on the following day. According to schedule, the Archduke and his wife were to leave Ilidže by special train at 9.25 am. They would be met at Sarajevo by six open cars. They would inspect a nearby barracks. At 10 sharp they would drive along the quayside of the River Miljacka to the town hall. There the Archduke would receive an address. After this, the procession of cars would drive through the narrow streets of the old town to the museum, where the Archduke would

officially open a new wing. There was a good deal more to the programme which was never carried out. Ilić had also made his dispositions: three conspirators on the river side of the quay, three on the land side, with himself unarmed to watch what was happening.

The conspirators were in their places by 9 am. The Archduke was also punctual. The only slip occurred at Sarajevo station where the leading automobile, which was supposed to be occupied by security officers from Vienna, drove off without them. The Archduke visited the barracks, and the drive along the quay then began. Of the six conspirators, five failed to do anything. They had never experienced a moving target and were also taken aback by the crowds. The first boy imagined that there was a policeman behind him and that, if he tried to pull out his bomb, the plot would be revealed. The second felt sorry for the Archduke's wife. Čabrinović, the third, was regarded as the least reliable and had only been given a bomb at the last moment. However, he was the only one to act. He asked a policeman: 'Which is His Majesty's car?' The policeman obligingly told him. He then knocked the detonator off against a lamp-post and threw his bomb.

The detonator hit the Archduke's wife on the neck and bruised her. The bomb landed on the back of the Archduke's car, bounced off, and exploded under the next car, damaging a wheel and injuring a dozen people. The damaged car was pushed out of the way, and the procession went on. Princip, hearing the explosion, left his post and saw Čabrinović being taken away. He thought of killing Čabrinović in order to keep the secret of the conspiracy, decided it was too difficult, and sat down in a café, contemplating suicide. The fifth boy was too shortsighted to see the Archduke and in any case lost his nerve. The last of them was still puzzling whether to follow Ilić's earlier instruction and call off the attempt. Also he feared that his bomb might injure people in the crowd. He, too, did absolutely nothing.

The second successful attempt

The Archduke arrived at the town hall in a bad temper. He said to the mayor: 'I come on a friendly visit, and someone throws a bomb at me.' Then, recovering himself, he listened to the mayor's address and made a more or less gracious answer. The Archduke asked Potiorek: 'Do you think other attempts will be made?' Potiorek answered: 'Go at ease. I accept all responsibility.' The Arch-

Left: The first attempt at assassination, which failed: a policeman stands beside the spot on the quayside where Čabrinović's bomb exploded under the car following that of the Archduke and injured a dozen people. Franz Ferdinand was on his way to visit them in hospital when the second attempt was made successfully

duke decided to visit the wounded men in hospital before going to the museum. The procession would therefore drive straight down the quay instead of turning into the old town. Count Harrach, who had lent his car to the Archduke for the day, stood on the running-board to ward off any further bombs from the river side. The drivers had not been told of the change of plan. The first two cars turned into the old town. The Archduke's driver followed them. Potiorek called out: 'Stop! You are going the wrong way.' The driver stopped and began to back into the quay.

Princip was sitting in the café exactly at this corner. To his astonishment, he saw the Archduke immediately before him. He pulled out his revolver. A policeman tried to strike up his hand and was kicked on the knee by a friend of Princip's who was standing by. Princip fired twice. One shot hit the Archduke. The other, perhaps intended for Potiorek who was sitting at the front, hit the Archduke's wife who was sitting at the back. She died at once. The Archduke murmured: 'Sophie, live for the children'; then: 'It is nothing' and fell back dead also.

Princip, like Čabrinović, was arrested. Both talked freely, and all but one of the other conspirators were soon arrested, along with many who had helped them to cross the frontier. After a laboriously fair trial, all those who were of age were sentenced to death. Čabrinović, Princip, and one other died in prison during the war, more from neglect than from ill-treatment. The other two were released after the war. One became curator of the Sarajevo museum; the other professor of history at Belgrade. The one who had escaped later returned to Sarajevo and ran a market garden. The Archduke and his wife were buried on his private estate without imperial honours. There were other victims. In 1917 Pašić framed Apis who was with the Serbian army at Salonika. Apis tried to save his associates by claiming that he had organised the Sarajevo assassination. This did not save him or them. They were all shot on a trumped-up charge.

Such was the spark which fired the First World War. It is ironical that it would not have gone off if the Archduke had stuck to his time-table. There was to be no further deviation.

*Right: The end of the antagonists of Sarajevo. Franz Ferdinand and his wife lie in state **(near right)** before being buried on his private estate without imperial honours: while Princip, the man who fired the first shot in the First World War, is led away **(top right)** to face trial with his companions **(bottom right)**. All the conspirators who were of age were shot while Čabrinović and Princip were to die in prison during the war*

Chapter 3
Decision in Vienna

An imperial power must do something when the heir to its throne is assassinated. That was obvious to everyone in Europe. The Habsburg monarchy had been losing prestige for a long time. Now it had a wonderful chance to assert itself. All the peoples of the monarchy except the Serbs demonstrated their loyalty with enthusiasm — the Hungarians, who had no reason to regret Franz Ferdinand, as enthusiastically as any other. The crowned heads of Europe were indignant at the killing of one of their number. A strong line by Austria-Hungary would meet with universal approval. But what line? The trial of the conspirators, even reprisals against the Serbs of Bosnia, were not enough. Something had to be done against Serbia herself.

Austrian officials looked for proof of Serbian complicity in the assassination. They never found any. They did not get on to the Black Hand at all, and in any case Princip's connection with it was tenuous. The reason for Austrian ignorance of the Black Hand was curious. In 1908 Austrian Intelligence had blundered. Forgách, the minister in Belgrade, acquired evidence of treasonable behaviour by Serbo-Croat leaders in Zagreb. The evidence turned out to be forged — some of it in the basement of Forgách's own house. Henceforth the Austrians relied on German Intelligence in Serbia, not on their own; and the Germans derived much of their information, in the agreeable way of Intelligence services, from none other than Apis. Naturally he did not mention the Black Hand.

Evidence was a secondary affair in any case. Serbia's real crime in Habsburg eyes was to exist. Serbia did not need to enlist conspirators. She kept the Serbs, and to a lesser extent the Croats, of Austria-Hungary in a turmoil merely by representing the national principle. There was no solution short of Serbia ceasing to exist, and this was impossible. The Serbs could not be exterminated, as might have happened in a more barbaric age or as Hitler might have attempted later. Annexation of Serbia to Austria-Hungary was equally impossible, even if the other powers

Left: Austrian officers demonstrate their loyalty to the emperor

had allowed it: it would merely have added more to Franz Joseph's discontented subjects. Humiliation of Serbia was the only answer. If the Habsburg monarchy displayed its might, it would temporarily restore its prestige.

Theoretically, the decision lay with Franz Joseph himself. He had so arranged the successive constitutional concessions of his reign that he kept foreign policy in his own hands. There was no Austro-Hungarian government. Occasionally, Franz Joseph held a gathering of the common ministers and other dignitaries, but this meeting only advised — it had no powers. In practice, Franz Joseph left foreign affairs to his foreign minister, who in 1914 was Count Berchtold, a rich Bohemian Count, formal in manner, smart in appearance, short in ideas and resolution. Berchtold consulted Forgách, now running Balkan affairs at the foreign ministry. Forgách was naturally for strong action against the Serbs who had deceived and humiliated him. Berchtold next consulted Conrad, chief of the general staff. Conrad, too, was for war, as he was on every occasion. But he explained, to Berchtold's dismay, that the peacetime forces, even if strong enough to deal with Serbia, could not be moved. Their movement would cut across the plans for mobilisation and make them unworkable. Austria-Hungary would therefore be helpless in case of a threat from Russia or even of powerful Serbian resistance. The time-tables dictated that there must be full mobilisation or nothing. Finally Berchtold consulted Tisza, prime minister of Hungary and the most forceful character in the monarchy. Tisza disliked the Serbs, but he did not fear them. He was much more fearful that a successful action against the Serbs would restore Habsburg prestige, to Hungary's disadvantage. He insisted that action should be taken only if Germany approved.

This suited Berchtold. He could demonstrate to his ally that Austria-Hungary did not merit the reproaches of feebleness levelled against her. At the same time, he could shift the responsibility for decision on to someone else. He drafted a note that Serbia 'must be eliminated as a power factor in the Balkans' and sent it to Berlin by special messenger. In Germany, too, there was no imperial government — only the Kaiser Wilhelm II and such ministers as he chose to consult. Wilhelm was at Potsdam, where the Austrian ambassador came for lunch on 5th July. Wilhelm did not hesitate. He was upset by the assassination of the archduke, who had been within the imperial limits a friend of his. His first reactions, though not his later ones, were always violent. Wilhelm at once agreed that Austria-Hungary should act against Serbia. He also promised that Germany would stand by Austria-Hungary if Russia tried to intervene. In after years, these seemed shocking things to say. They were natural and

inevitable in the atmosphere of the time. No crowned head, the German Emperor least of all, could have told the Austrians that they should disregard the Archduke's assassination. No German statesman at this moment, and least of all the Emperor, could have left Austria-Hungary at the mercy of Russia. German diplomats had complained for years past that Austria-Hungary had been fearful and irresolute. Here for once the Austrians were trying to be firm, and Germany could do no other than encourage them.

Bethmann backs the Kaiser

Wilhelm showed more sense in the course of the afternoon. He consulted such German generals as happened to be available and asked them whether this was a suitable moment to back Austria-Hungary. The available generals were mostly court officials. They had picked up from more serious military authorities talk about a preventive war. They agreed that this was a good, even a desirable, moment for war. Wilhelm also insisted that he could make no firm decision without the approval of his chancellor, Bethmann Hollweg — a most admirable respect for constitutional principle. Bethmann arrived at Potsdam in the course of the afternoon. In character and perhaps in intellect he was ranked above most other statesmen of the day. He played Beethoven where Berchtold went to the races and Grey went fishing. In his grave appearance there was an impressive sense of responsibility. During past alarms he had sometimes restrained Wilhelm II, and he often tried to lessen the roughness of German policy. On the other hand he had got into his head the idea that Germany was about to run downhill. Like the generals who talked of preventive war, Bethmann believed that it was 'now or never'. There seems a special disease among statesmen which makes them feel that their highly prosperous country is on the brink of ruin. Bethmann had this disease strongly.

Bethmann knew, before he left for Potsdam, that the question of Austro-Hungarian policy and of Germany's attitude towards it would come up. Yet he made no preparations. Jagow, the secretary of state, was away on holiday, and Bethmann did not seek advice from anyone else in the foreign ministry. Nor did he enquire of the general staff — a practice he had never followed. His lack of precise information did not, however, deter him. As soon as Wilhelm had outlined his answer to the Austrians, Bethmann endorsed it. This was not from timidity or subservience. Indeed Bethmann provided some new arguments of his to show how strongly he agreed with his

Left: Tisza, 'the most forceful character in the monarchy'

imperial master. He, too, had little appreciation of what he was doing. It seemed obvious to him that Austria-Hungary should be supported and equally obvious that Russia would make no effective protest. Confidence that Russia would back down at the last moment had become a habit with German diplomats, and Bethmann had no means of knowing whether Russian resolution or the state of Russian armaments might have changed. He guessed blindly in the void. There was a sort of competition in 'dares' — what the Americans call playing chicken. First the Austrians showed how brave they were to talk of going to war and dared the Germans to restrain them. Now the Germans showed how brave they were by encouraging the Austrians and so dared the Austrians to pull back. Vienna wanted to impress Berlin. Berlin wanted to impress Vienna. No one in either capital seriously contemplated the chances of general war.

After the momentous conversations at Potsdam, Wilhelm II went on holiday, and most of the generals departed also. This was not an act of deception. Wilhelm II and the rest assumed that somehow war could be fitted in between a couple of vacations. Though they had talked of war, they could not imagine it. Their only military experience was on manoeuvres, where action could be conveniently broken off at dinner time. Wilhelm II and Bethmann soon forgot, or very nearly, the formidable promises which they had made to Austria-Hungary. If they recalled these promises at all it was with the consoling reflection that the Austrians never stuck to any firm resolution for long. Thus the two men who were responsible for German policy gave Berchtold a blank cheque, told him to fill it in for a large sum, and yet were confident that he would not present it at all.

They were very nearly right. Berchtold was enthusiastic for war only so long as he knew that someone would restrain him. He became more and more hesitant as the obstacles to war disappeared. When the German encouragements arrived in Vienna, even Tisza wavered. If the German rulers thought Austria-Hungary should go to war, then perhaps the risk was worth while. Tisza disputed the necessity for war over nearly a week. Finally he yielded, because of the need to come up to German expectations. But he still made a condition: Austria-Hungary should not acquire any Serbian territory, however great the victory of her arms. Berchtold agreed to this condition though it made nonsense of his policy. For there was no purpose in war if Serbia was to be merely harassed, not dismembered. By this time, Berchtold had lost his enthusiasm for war, and the staff in the foreign

Left: The Emperor Franz Joseph and one of his devoted retainers

ministry at the Ballhausplatz shared his hesitations. As one of them wrote later, they were like 'someone who is to undergo an operation and hopes more or less confidently to be able to escape it'. Forgotten were the days when Berchtold was pushing Tisza into war. Now Berchtold was finding excuses why war should be postponed.

Austria-Hungary waits and wonders

The European powers might have tolerated an immediate stroke against Serbia in the first flush of indignation. All idea of this had long been abandoned. In true bureaucratic fashion, the Austrian diplomats wished to justify their own prejudices and laboriously sought evidence that the Serbian government had been involved. A legal official was sent to Belgrade. After a couple of days, he reported correctly that there was no evidence against the Serbian government. This was irrelevant, though slightly awkward. The Austrians had resolved to act somehow against Serbia for reasons remote from the Archduke's assassination. Their real problem was in drafting the ultimatum. They had to devise conditions which would bring some sort of advantage, even though their real aim was that Serbia would reject them. By 14th July the note was ready. Ministers came to Berchtold's private house secretly at night in order to discuss it. Apparently they wanted to give the impression that nothing was happening. Berchtold himself was by now hoping that nothing would happen. Even if Serbia did not accept the Austro-Hungarian demands, she might well do so when faced by a mobilisation – a dream project to which Berchtold had reverted, even though Conrad had told him that it was impossible.

A new pretext for delay now emerged. President Poincaré of France was on the point of visiting St Petersburg along with Viviani, who combined the posts of French premier and foreign minister. It would never do for the Russian and French statesmen to discuss the Austro-Hungarian note face to face. Presentation of the note was therefore put off until Poincaré and Viviani left St Petersburg for the voyage home. In this way, almost a month passed. The Archduke had been assassinated. Austria-Hungary took no action, even diplomatic. The question was not quite forgotten in the other European capitals, but it lost any sense of urgency. Most people assumed that the Austrians would do nothing serious in their usual ineffective way. 71 ▷

Right: Even when war came it was reflected in glamorous colour and glamorous uniforms. Gaily drawn bonds in a Russian armaments firm (top right). Austrian infantryman idealised (bottom right). Fine feathers: Franz Joseph and Wilhelm II (near right). Next page: Austrian dignitaries ignore the impending storm

The other powers could not decide on a policy until Austria-Hungary did something, but the Russians at any rate did some thinking. Sazonov, the Russian foreign minister, was a gentle, puzzled man, not very bright, with a romantic Slav devotion to his duty. He had been admirably cautious during the Balkan wars and now asked nothing better than that the Balkans should be left to the Balkan peoples. Pan-Slavs may once have dreamt of extending Russian power into the Balkans. Now Russia's anxiety was that no European great power should control the Bosphorus and the Dardanelles—Russia's outlet to the world. Through these straits Russian wheat went out to pay her debts, and steel and machinery for her heavy industry came in. Without security at the straits, Russia could hardly exist as a great power. The Russians feared rightly that Germany was building up influence in Turkey. They also feared with less justification that this influence would be used to close the straits against them.

The prospect of Austro-Hungarian domination over Serbia threw the Russians into a state of alarm. They imagined that this would bring Germany that much nearer to Constantinople. This was a misconception. Germany's economic route to Turkey was by sea—from Hamburg or Rotterdam, and the Balkans meant nothing to her. Even Austria-Hungary's interest was mainly political, except for the railway line to Salonika. But if Allied statesmen during the First World War, such as Churchill, could imagine that Constantinople and the Balkans provided a backdoor into Germany, the Russians may be forgiven for believing beforehand that the backdoor could be used the other way round. There were simpler impulses at work in Sazonov's mind. Russia was no longer a despotism. The Liberal politicians now counted for something, and they would be offended if nothing was done to uphold the Slav cause.

The French statesmen were more remotely involved. The prospect of a general European war was the least of their worries. They were far more anxious that Russia might quarrel with Great Britain over Persia and then abandon the Triple Entente in favour of Germany. Hence they stressed their own loyalty to the Russian alliance—exactly as Wilhelm II and Bethmann had stressed their loyalty to the Austro-German alliance. At least, this was Poincaré's view. In normal circumstances, the French President had little to say in foreign policy. But the circumstances were not normal. Viviani, though foreign minister, was merely the stop-gap premier of a Radical-Socialist coalition, the real leader, Caillaux, being temporarily out of the running because his wife had just shot

Left: Fashionable Berchtold greets less fashionable Bethmann

71

and killed a Parisian newspaper editor. Viviani knew nothing of foreign affairs and left them to Poincaré. However there is no evidence that the Russian and French statesmen ever discussed the Serbian affair. It was fourteenth on the agenda which the French had brought with them and was never reached. Of course Poincaré talked about the glories of the Franco-Russian alliance and gave the Russians general encouragement. But his real concern was to keep Russia on good terms with Great Britain.

'To Hell with Servia'

The British were the least involved at all. Even the few who feared that the Archduke's assassination might provoke a war did not foresee that Great Britain would be involved in it. Serbia had a bad press in Great Britain. 'The least worthy member of the European family' was the general verdict. The *Manchester Guardian* wished that Serbia could be towed out to sea and sunk. Horatio Bottomley, the demagogue, produced the headline: 'To Hell with Servia.' Sir Edward Grey, the Foreign Secretary, took the same line more decorously. In his view, peace was more important than justice, and the lesser power must yield, however humiliatingly, so that peace could be preserved. This was the usual British outlook — repeated with Greece in 1923 and with Czechoslovakia in 1938. Of course Grey issued warnings against any violent action. He talked vaguely of mediation, but who between? If between Serbia and Austria-Hungary, the Austrians would reject any outside interference, and Grey, as foreign secretary of a great power which had often disciplined some small one, would be inclined to agree with them. If the suggested mediation was to be between Austria-Hungary and Russia, the Austrians could reply with equal plausibility that Russia was not involved. Until Austria-Hungary acted in some way, the Russians could not react, and it was of course easy to assume that, since the Austrians had taken one month to think of an action, the Russians would take another to think of an answer.

It was a strange crisis — everyone waiting for some sort of explosion, with the Serbian government waiting most anxiously of all. They were in bad trouble: their army was exhausted by the Balkan wars and they knew that, whatever happened, Serbia could not gain. They were also without a trusted counsellor. For years past they had relied on Hartvig, the Russian minister in Belgrade. On 10th July they lost him under strange circumstances. Hartvig, once an extremist, was now a moderate. He called on the Austro-Hungarian minister in

Right: Diffident allies, Sazonov and Poincaré on the march

order to propose a common front against nationalist conspirators such as the Black Hand. The excitement was too much for him. In the middle of making his proposal, which would no doubt have prevented the war, he fell dead. Russia was virtually unrepresented thereafter. The Russian government received no information, and the Serbian government received little advice.

On 23rd July President Poincaré ended his state visit to St Petersburg. The Austrians had ascertained the precise moment when the French cruiser, taking him home, would cast off. One hour afterwards, Giesl, the Austro-Hungarian minister at Belgrade, presented his government's ultimatum. This was tight timing. The Serbs were given forty-eight hours in which to reply. By then, 6.00 pm on 25th July, it would be Saturday evening, and the Austrians wanted to start mobilising on the Sunday morning. The Serbian government were summoned to repudiate the nationalist societies and to proceed against those accessories to the assassination who were on Serb soil — Austrian officials were to collaborate in this. There were ten points in all, but the collaboration of Austrian officials seemed the essential one. If the Serbian government agreed to this, it would be confessing its inability to keep assassins under control. Even so, the agreement was very nearly given.

Pašić, the Prime Minister, had left on an election tour when the Austrian note arrived. Evidently he hoped to escape responsibility for decision one way or the other. When summoned to return, he left for a holiday in Greece and had to be pulled off the train to receive a telegram of recall from the Prince Regent. By the time he got back, the Serbian ministers had decided to accept the Austrian demands almost unconditionally. There were slight changes of phrasing so as to imply the innocence of the Serbian government. Even so, it would have been almost impossible for the Austrians to declare that their terms had not been met. They would have had to make do with boasting instead of war. Acceptance of such terms would be humiliating for Serbia. It would weaken national enthusiasm for the time being. But Serbia would survive and be free to resume the South Slav cause later.

At the last minute the Serbian ministers changed their minds. They decided to make difficulties over some of the Austrian demands and to reject the collaboration with Austrian officials outright. It is not known what swung them round. Pašić may have feared that Austrian officials would find out about the Black Hand. The Sarajevo investigation had already uncovered Tankosić, and **78** ▷

Left: Russian workers, far from the glitter of the Tsar's court
Next page: *Nicholas II and his council of ministers hard at work*

from him the trail led straight to Apis. Perhaps Pašić was himself threatened by the Black Hand. A more popular hypothesis claims that there was some message from St Petersburg, urging the Serbian government to stand firm. The written record fails us. However, there was one Russian action, or preliminary to action, which spoke louder than words.

Russia gets involved

On 24th July, when first news of the Austro-Hungarian ultimatum came through, Sazonov urged on the Tsar and the council of ministers that Russia could not stand entirely aside. She must show that she was involved. But how? An immediate protest to Vienna would be too provocative, especially when it was not known whether the Serbs intended to refuse the Austrian demands. A promise of support in Belgrade would commit Russia too much. But what about a mobilisation in the military districts adjacent to Austria-Hungary? This would show that Russia was not sleeping. At the same time, it would be an assurance that towards Germany Russia had no warlike intentions. Sazonov's colleagues were delighted with the idea. It seemed to offer exactly what they wanted: a gesture of support for Serbia without firm commitment or risk of general war. Sazonov did not consult the chief-of-staff or any other military spokesman. If he had done, he would have learnt that this partial mobilisation was unworkable – it would cut across the plans for general mobilisation and make them impossible. It could be tried only if there were a firm pledge of German neutrality, and that was not likely to happen. However, the chief-of-staff had not been long in office and did not venture to wrangle with the foreign minister. Sazonov went on believing he had a safe weapon when he cared to use it.

For the moment, the Russian government were content to take only preliminary steps – recall of technical officers and so on; seemingly harmless though involving nearly a million men by the end of the month. The Serbians seem to have learnt Sazonov's further intentions. Here was an assurance that Serbia would not be left totally friendless. The prospect stirred the Serbians to more resolute behaviour. Unless they showed their spirit, Russia might shift her favour to some other Balkan country. Though still anxious to avoid war, the Serbian ministers walked a little nearer the edge. They aimed to keep the dispute with Austria-Hungary going so that, in the subsequent diplomatic wrangling, Russian prestige could be asserted. Throughout Saturday, 25th July, the Serbian ministers worked on their answer, inserting reservations on the original typescript until the last moment. The changes of phrase were sometimes

plausibly conciliatory, sometimes insolent. The refusal to admit Austrian officials at the Serb enquiry was the only point which gave excuse for a breach.

The Serbian ministers also decided to mobilise the army and to withdraw the government to Niš, further from the Austro-Hungarian frontier. Pašić himself delivered the answer at the Austro-Hungarian legation with five minutes to spare, at 5.55 pm. He then caught the official train to Niš, also by a narrow margin. Giesl took a quick look at the Serbian note; saw that it was not an unconditional acceptance; and at once sent back a note he had already prepared, announcing that he was leaving Belgrade and that diplomatic relations between Austria-Hungary and Serbia were broken off. He was just in time to catch the 6.30 pm train from Belgrade and ten minutes later was on Hungarian soil. He telephoned to Tisza who asked: 'Did it have to be?' Giesl answered: 'Yes.' His news was telegraphed to Vienna. Franz Joseph was on holiday at Ischl, where Berchtold had joined him. Giesl's news was telegraphed on to them. When Franz Joseph learnt it, he remarked untranslatably: 'Also doch' – meaning something like: 'Berchtold told me things would not go wrong, but they have.' He added: 'However, breaking off diplomatic relations does not necessarily mean war.' Berchtold's comments are not recorded. When the news arrived, he was out taking a walk. Later in the evening he persuaded Franz Joseph to sign the order for mobilisation against Serbia. But he shared much of Franz Joseph's optimism and added the further consolation: 'Mobilisation does not mean war.'

Berchtold's resolution was by now exhausted. This silly gentleman had never intended to go to war. He had been assured by everyone from Forgách to Wilhelm II that if he showed an unshakable spirit Serbia would at some point give way – perhaps when the Austrian note was presented, perhaps when relations were broken off, or perhaps with the threat of Austro-Hungarian mobilisation. Berchtold had little desire to go further. The bluff, to which others had encouraged him, was not succeeding and, in the usual way of those who get into this position, he proposed to play for time, in other words to do nothing. This was not a bad idea. The other powers still had no desire to be involved in war for Serbia's sake. Both Sazonov and Grey were tumbling over themselves to get Berchtold out of his mess. 25th July was of course a Saturday, and it was too much to expect that Sir Edward Grey would give up his weekend's fishing for a remote Balkan crisis. However, he approved a suggestion from the Foreign Office that Great Britain should propose an

Left: Farewell Russian style as the first mobilisations begin

international conference similar to the ambassadors' meetings during the Balkan wars. At the same time, Sazonov was cutting across this proposal by seeking direct talks with Austria-Hungary.

Both proposals were made to Germany, on the assumption that Bethmann, like Grey and Sazonov, was anxious to avoid war. This assumption was mistaken. Bethmann probably wanted to avoid a general European war. On the other hand, he consciously wanted a 'localised' war — that is, a war between Austria-Hungary and Serbia. This, he thought, would solve all his problems. It would restore Austro-Hungarian prestige. It would demonstrate Germany's loyalty to her ally and so increase her prestige also. The conciliatory pleadings from Sazonov and Grey convinced him that neither of them would go to war merely for the sake of Serbia, and the lack of any decisive French policy while Poincaré and Viviani were still absent strengthened his confidence. But he was in a hurry. The statesmen of the Entente powers might change their minds. Still worse, Wilhelm II was returning home against Bethmann's advice, and he, as Bethmann well knew, was likely to turn soft when faced with a real danger of war. This indeed was exactly what happened. As soon as he got back, he declared that the Serbian answer was a triumph for Vienna and ought to have been accepted. His conversion was too late. By then, Bethmann's insistence had pushed Austria-Hungary into war.

Berchtold was repeatedly prodded by urgings from Berlin. Grey's proposals for mediation or an international conference were sent on to him belatedly, with an assurance that Germany had already turned them down, but also with a warning that they could not be resisted indefinitely. Austria-Hungary must present Europe with a *fait accompli*. Grey must be met with the answer: 'Too late.' Berchtold summoned Conrad, the chief-of-staff. An odd situation was revealed. The timid pacific diplomat wanted to declare war. The fire-eating general was against it. Conrad explained that mobilisation, even against Serbia, would take some time. The Austro-Hungarian army could not be ready until 12th August, and a declaration of war before then would expose it to derision. This was music in Berchtold's ears. A declaration of war would after all mean nothing. It would be merely another diplomatic move, a further gesture of bluff which might make the Serbs give way. Meanwhile he would have displayed his own resolve anew and would have satisfied his German ally. He rejected Conrad's advocacy of 12th August with the words: 'The diplomatic situation will not hold so long.'

Right: *Unsuspecting Russian officers at their most industrious*

Berchtold, now back in Vienna, wired Franz Joseph at Ischl that Serbian troops had fired on the Austrians. Franz Joseph wired back his approval of a declaration of war on Serbia. By this time, the report of the Serbian troops having opened fire had turned out to be false. Berchtold struck the reference to it out of the declaration of war, though he did not inform Franz Joseph of this until after the declaration had gone. In later years Berchtold asserted that he had not intended to deceive his imperial master, so perhaps duplicity had merely become a habit with him. One problem remained: how to deliver the declaration of war, in view of the fact that relations had already been broken off. The Germans, who were looking after Austro-Hungarian interests in Serbia, refused to act as postmen, since, in Jagow's words, 'it might give the impression that we had hounded Austria-Hungary into war.' However, Berchtold or his officials found a simple answer. The declaration of war was sent to Belgrade by the ordinary telegraph via Bucharest.

Pašić received the telegram at 1 pm on 28th July. He thought it might be an Austrian trick, designed to provoke a Serbian attack. He telegraphed to the Serbian ministers at London, Paris, and St Petersburg, asking whether Austria-Hungary had really declared war on Serbia. The answers came back during the afternoon. It was true. The war had started, at any rate in theory. But nothing real seemed to have happened. Berchtold was soon saying that a declaration of war was not the same as war, and events almost proved him right. There was no serious fighting between Serbia and Austria-Hungary until the autumn of 1914, when Potiorek, in command, mismanaged the invasion of Serbia as badly as he had mismanaged the Archduke's visit to Sarajevo. Yet war, even ineffective and unfought, was basically different from the sternest diplomatic threats. The great powers had waged plenty of wars with countries outside Europe and with one, Turkey, on the fringe. But no great power had issued a declaration of war against another European country since 1870. Berchtold did not mean to start a war, even against Serbia. He merely wanted to show that he was not an impossibly weak foreign minister and to find some means of stopping the flow of reproaches, rebukes, and proddings which came to him from Berlin. Having deceived everyone in turn – Tisza, Conrad, Franz Joseph, the Germans, the Entente statesmen – he ended by deceiving himself. But what Berchtold intended or desired was no longer of importance. By declaring war on Serbia, Berchtold fired the second shot in the First World War as surely, if as unintentionally, as Princip fired the first.

Right: Waiting and practising, Russian artillery in barracks

Chapter 4
Decision in Berlin

Men in Vienna started a Balkan war or at least made the gesture of doing so. This was the utmost they were capable of. It depended on the rulers of the really great powers whether this would grow into a European war, and it depended most of all on men in Berlin. All the others were eager to compromise. The British and French cared nothing at all for Serbia. Even the Russians were willing that Austria-Hungary should obtain some satisfaction, though not all she sought. There was a way out which, curiously enough, was grasped most clearly by a man in Potsdam, if not in Berlin. Wilhelm II had lost his bellicose ardour. He remained convinced that the Serbian reply gave Austria-Hungary all she needed. His erratic intellect pointed to a solution. The Austrians should occupy Belgrade as a pledge that Serbia would fulfil her promises. At the same time, they would declare that they had no designs against Serbian sovereignty. This was the Halt in Belgrade, a solution which any capable diplomat might have devised and which could have ended the crisis.

The Austrians did not like it. They hesitated to move against Serbia until 12th August when their mobilisation would be theoretically complete. Ironically their apprehensions were unfounded. The Serbs had resolved not to defend Belgrade, and the Austrians could have occupied it almost without firing a shot. They had a larger objection. Once war with Serbia really started, the Austrians did not intend to keep their promise of respecting Serbian integrity. If Tisza's objections could be overcome, Austria-Hungary herself would annex Serbian territory; if not, chunks of it could be thrown to Bulgaria and Albania. Later events were to make the object look foolish. For, in the autumn of 1914, it was the Serbs who ended in occupation of Hungarian territory and not the other way round. Such however were the calculations which led Berchtold to turn a deaf ear to all projects for a halt in Belgrade.

Left: Kaiser Wilhelm remembers the triumphs of a former war: commemorating the Battle of the Nations at Leipzig in 1813

Berchtold's evasions and silences mattered little. The decisive opposition to William II's conciliatory diplomacy came from Bethmann, who displayed a surprising disregard for his imperial master except when it suited him. Bethmann was obstinately set on a localised war. All along he had wanted a violent reassertion of Austro-Hungarian prestige, with German support, so that the standing of the Central Powers would be increased. If Austria-Hungary compromised or weakened, Germany's prestige would be shaken also. Bethmann was convinced that Serbia would yield at some point, preferably after a war. He was also committed to the doctrine that Russia would not intervene, if faced with the threat of war with Germany. He had laid down this doctrine on 5th July. He continued to hold it on 28th July. He had virtually no choice. For if Russia failed to back down, what happened to the belief in Germany's strong right arm? What would be said by all the patriotic Germans who had been told for a generation that their army was the most powerful in the world? Bethmann liked to think that he acted as a brake on German nationalism, and of course a brake can work only when the vehicle is moving. A check, if not a humiliation, for Russia was an essential part of Bethmann's policy.

Bethmann begins to get muddled

Bethmann had a secondary aim which gradually moved up to first place. His constant refrain had been: 'War will be averted if Germany stands firm. But if war comes after all, the responsibility for it must lie with Russia.' In his anxiety to shift the blame on to Russia, Bethmann came almost to forget his original objective. Putting the blame on to Russia had for Bethmann great attractions. Russian initiative might make the French hesitate, as they had done during the Bosnian crisis. More important from Bethmann's point of view, it would keep Great Britain neutral — or so Bethmann believed. Bethmann was not thinking in terms of armies, where the British counted but little. Perhaps he doubted whether the German army could win at a single blow and therefore looked forward to a long war. More probably, as a conservative but civilised German, Bethmann regarded Great Britain as his touchstone and needed her neutrality to maintain his psychological confidence.

Bethmann had also a domestic calculation. As Chancellor, he tried to straddle between Left and Right.

*Far left: Contrasting comments on the failures of the statesmen: the ghost of Bismarck visits Wilhelm II (top), while peaceful Germany is threatened by Russian aggression (bottom).
Near left: One of the first men to be mobilised girds himself*

Though himself conservative, he hoped for a time when the Social Democrats, now the largest single party in the Reichstag, would join the government side instead of remaining permanently in opposition. The process was already happening. Though still theoretically Marxist internationalists, the German Social Democrats were, in fact, becoming day-to-day opportunists with a strong dose of German sentiment. A threat from Russia would push them over the edge. They had made an exception about Russia in their anti-war principles from the days of Marx and Engels onwards. Bebel, their leader, had declared long ago: 'Against Russia the Social Democrats would march as one man.' Thus, if the situation could be presented as a Russian aggression against Germany, Bethmann would accomplish the miracle which had escaped every German statesman since 1848. He would produce a united Germany, and so he did.

A tame ending to the crisis was therefore unwelcome to Bethmann. It was easy for him to run Wilhelm II's well-meaning efforts into the sand. Wilhelm II was at Potsdam and absurdly had no telephone line to Berlin. Every message from him had to be delivered by hand, and each time Bethmann was able to reply that it was too late. It had been superseded by events. Similarly, William II only learnt of diplomatic developments some hours after they had happened. At a time when every minute counted, the most powerful ruler in Europe was always a day behind events.

The time-tables take command

The situation was moving faster than Bethmann or anyone else expected. By declaring war against Serbia, the Austrians had turned everything upside down. Where previously they had drifted with intolerable slowness, they had now fixed a final date, 12th August, before which everything must be settled or get out of hand. Even this date soon proved too far ahead. Berchtold assumed that he had a fortnight in hand before anything real happened. Conrad shattered this illusion. He explained that until 1st August mobilisation could proceed against Serbia alone. On that day he must decide whether to continue mobilising solely against Serbia or whether, as provided by his flexible planning, the remaining four army corps should be directed towards the Russian front. In other words, Austria-Hungary must have a guarantee of Russian neutrality by 1st August. The Austrians could not obtain this themselves, for any approach to Russia by them would imply a recognition that their dealings with Serbia were not a simple localised war. It was time, in fact, for Germany to fulfil her promise and to keep Russia neutral by threat of war.

At exactly the same time the Russians were facing the need for decision. They had resolved to give Serbia support which they still hoped would be only diplomatic. They did not know that the Austrians dared not go on with their mobilisation against Serbia without a guarantee of Russian neutrality. On the contrary, the Russians assumed that they, too, must negotiate arms in hand. It never occurred to them that, merely by doing nothing, they could prevent Austria-Hungary's acting against Serbia or, at worst, compel Germany to act openly as the aggressor – which Bethmann was determined not to do. The most difficult thing in a crisis is to wait upon events, and the Russians could not bring themselves to do it. Uncertainty weighed them down and, as well, Sazonov, like others, wished to show that he was not the weak, irresolute character that he was alleged to be – and was.

Sazonov believed that there was still a safe way out: a partial Russian mobilisation directed solely against Austria-Hungary. Grey had telegraphed that he found this quite natural. Jagow, the German secretary of state, had said on 26th July that Germany would make no objection. Here was the secret card on which Sazonov had relied all along. On 28th July he learnt of the Austro-Hungarian declaration of war against Serbia and at once went to see Nicholas II at Peterhof, seventeen miles from St Petersburg. Sazonov produced his solution. The Russian generals objected. Now, and apparently not before, they explained that partial mobilisation was impossible. There were no plans prepared for it. It would be a hastily improvised operation. Still worse, once it began, general mobilisation would become impossible, and Russia would be at Germany's mercy. Nicholas II and Sazonov hesitated once more and finally decided to avoid a decision. Two orders or ukazes should be prepared – one for partial, one for general mobilisation. The further formalities were important. First the ukaze must be signed by the Tsar. Then it must be signed by the ministers for war and the navy. Finally the Tsar must again give his approval.

The next morning Sazonov, back in St Petersburg, had a discussion with Janushkevich, the chief-of-staff. He was shaken by the military arguments against partial mobilisation. He therefore agreed that Janushkevich should take both ukazes to Peterhof for the Tsar's signature, which Janushkevich did. Nicholas II signed both, without however finally committing himself to either. Janushkevich had no interest in the ukaze for partial mobilisation. Back in St Petersburg, he took the ukaze

Left: The first French reservists begin the march to the front

89

for general mobilisation to Sukhomlinov, minister for war, who declared that Russia was unready for war. Maklahov, the Minister of the Interior, who was also present, added that war would lead to revolution. Sukhomlinov exclaimed: 'We cannot escape our fate,' crossed himself, and signed the ukaze. Janushkevich took the ukaze on to the Minister for the Navy and then waited impatiently for the Tsar's final approval.

Bethmann loses his nerve

This was given and then snatched away again. In both cases the motive came from Berlin. On 29th July Bethmann began to lose his nerve. It became clear to him that, if Austria-Hungary went ahead against Serbia without any attempt at compromise, the diplomatic situation would not move in Germany's favour. Germany would have to threaten Russia and would be displayed as the aggressor. The Social Democrats would not be won over; Great Britain would not pledge her neutrality. Yet the German generals were insisting that, with the rumours of mobilisation coming out of Russia, German mobilisation could not long be delayed. Shortly after midday on 29th July Bethmann therefore sent a message to Sazonov that 'further progress of Russian mobilisation would compel us to mobilise'. This was meant as a warning, not as a threat. Bethmann did not grasp the difference between Russian partial and general mobilisation, which indeed to all military men was non-existent. But for Sazonov the message was shattering. It destroyed his faith that there was a way of checking Austria-Hungary without bringing on war with Germany.

Once more Sazonov conferred with the Russian military leaders. They again argued for general mobilisation, and now he agreed with them. After the message from Bethmann, the difference between partial and general mobilisation seemed to have disappeared. In this way, Sazonov, having been bewitched by the escape hatch of partial mobilisation, drifted into the general mobilisation which he had never intended to promote. The recommendation for general mobilisation was telephoned to **94** ▷

Left: Karl Liebknecht disguised as Martin Luther reproaches Kaiser Wilhelm II in an unlikely cartoon by Raemaekers. When war did come the German socialists came forward gladly to fight for their country against what was presented to them as Russian aggression, quietly forgetting all their previous talk of pacifism. Next page: Rarely had life been more glittering in France than in the period before the outbreak of war. But the determination of German statesmen that if they were to be involved in war then their first enemy must be France was to destroy all this. An artist depicts the gay summer scene as Paris began to mobilise and all rivalries were submerged in the preparations for war

Nicholas II, and he agreed to it. But both Nicholas II and Sazonov went on believing that they were merely increasing the bid, not committing themselves to war. The typewriters began to tap out the necessary telegrams. Later in the evening Nicholas received a telegram from his cousin, Wilhelm II. Wilhelm implied, sincerely though inaccurately, that his proposal for the Halt in Belgrade was within sight of accomplishment. Russian mobilisation, even against Austria-Hungary, would throw it out.

Nicholas II was shaken. Clad in his night-shirt, he stumbled downstairs in the empty palace and telephoned to Sukhomlinov that the general mobilisation should be stopped. He and Janushkevich tried to argue that this was impossible, but the Tsar answered: 'Stop it', and the generals prepared to obey. Transmission of military telegrams stopped for the night. Did the Tsar intend that partial mobilisation should be stopped also? Apparently not, for he wired back to Wilhelm II that the military measures now coming into force had been decided on for reasons of defence because of Austria's preparations. The generals however deplored partial mobilisation, so it may be that they in fact held up all action, while the Tsar presumed that partial mobilisation was going ahead.

The Tsar makes his decision

Sazonov made the same assumption, though he drew a different conclusion from it. After his prolonged discussions with the generals, he had now grasped that partial mobilisation was impossible. But, instead of abandoning all mobilisation for the moment, he became an advocate of general mobilisation. On the morning of 30th July, he telephoned the Tsar, who refused to be moved. Finally, the Tsar agreed to see Sazonov at three o'clock that afternoon. Once more Sazonov journeyed to Peterhof, bearing with him a message from the president of the Duma that 'as head of the representatives of the Russian people he would never forgive a delay which might precipitate the country into fatal confusion'. For over an hour Sazonov argued in vain. The Tsar would not commit himself to war. The Tsar's aide-de-camp said sympathetically: 'Yes, it is hard to decide.' The Tsar snapped: 'I will decide' and did so. He told Sazonov to authorise general mobilisation. Sazonov telephoned Janushkevich with the news and ended: 'Now you can smash your telephone.' The orders went out at 4 pm. The red call-up notices appeared on the walls during the night. Yet once again this was not

Right: Berlin, special edition containing the declaration of war is distributed by taxi. Popular clamour did not drive the great powers into war, it was only when the decisions had been taken that the crowds turned out to cheer and support their leaders

intended as a decision for war. Nicholas II believed correctly that the mobilised Russian armies could remain at their post for an indefinite time. On the following afternoon he promised Wilhelm II that Russian troops would not move so long as negotiations were going on between Austria-Hungary and Serbia. This promise was sincere and could have been kept.

The Austrians, however, did not mean to negotiate. They began to develop enthusiasm for a localised war just when others, including Bethmann, lost faith in it. Berchtold was timid so long as he was being pushed by the Germans. He developed a new obstinacy when Bethmann instead began to display doubts. By 30th July Bethmann had come round to the Halt in Belgrade. This was the moment when Berchtold resolved to wreck the idea. There was an obvious course for him to take. An Austro-Hungarian general mobilisation would be the repudiation of a localised war. It would imply that war with Russia was inevitable and so force Bethmann to abandon his belated attempts at conciliation. More practically, it would at last relieve Conrad's anxieties.

The soldiers take a hand

This new bellicosity by Berchtold received support from an unexpected source. Until now Moltke, the German chief-of-staff, had left diplomacy to Bethmann and in any case, knowing his own insufficiency, was anxious to avoid war. As the crisis deepened, he, too, wanted to show that he was a strong man. Moreover, it seemed that Wilhelm II, failing to get conciliatory answers from the Tsar, was also swinging round to violence again. Moltke therefore telegraphed to Conrad: 'Mobilise at once against Russia.' On the morning of 31st July, Conrad showed this telegram to Berchtold, who was himself waving the telegrams in an opposite sense from Bethmann. Berchtold exclaimed: 'That's rich. Who rules in Berlin: Moltke or Bethmann?' He decided to follow the Moltke line. Austro-Hungarian general mobilisation was proclaimed later in the morning. Neither the Russians nor the Austrians knew that the other had started general mobilisation. In this way, each provided justification for the other's act without knowing that they were doing so. But, as with Russian mobilisation, Austro-Hungarian mobilisation merely raised the tension. It was not a decision for a general war.

This decision was taken in Berlin on 31st July, and almost without debate. Bethmann had been told often enough by Moltke and others that mobilisation meant

Right: As the time-tables inexorably begin to turn mobilisation into war, German troops prepare to set off for the front

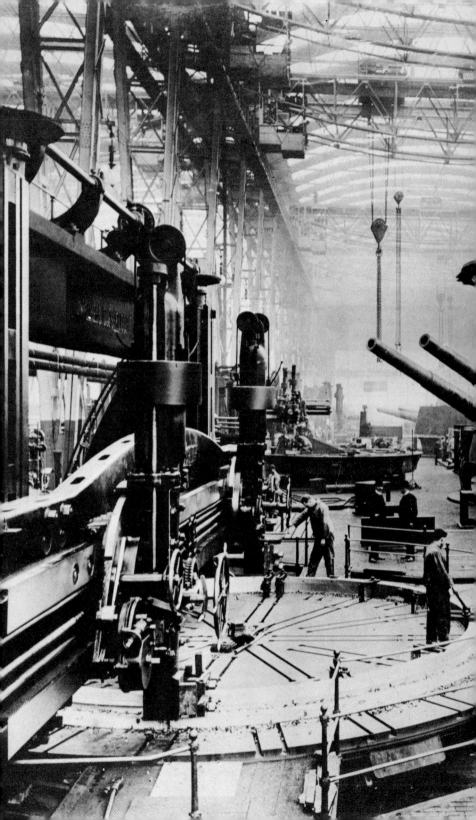

war, as indeed it did for Germany. He therefore assumed that the same was true for Russia and that with Russia's general mobilisation all hope for peace had vanished. His hope that Great Britain and perhaps even France would be estranged from Russia if she mobilised had been belied. Therefore he ceased to be interested in avoiding war and was concerned only to win it. Far from being pushed on by Moltke, Bethmann now wanted to know how quickly the Fatherland could go to war. Moltke, for his part, was bewitched by the time-table which he had inherited from Schlieffen. He was convinced that, once Russia started to mobilise, Germany could not waste a day. Yet he knew that Russian mobilisation would lurch along for many weeks and that Germany had plenty of time in hand. Instead he sounded the alarm of French mobilisation, which had, in fact, not yet started. Even this alarm was misplaced. For the object of the Schlieffen plan was to encircle the French armies in their advanced positions on the frontier. Therefore the more advanced and mobilised they were, the greater the catastrophe.

None of these calculations was made. With combined despair, Bethmann and Moltke hurried each other into war, both convinced that all chance of peace was over and both also believing, with a mixture of patriotic illusion and personal gloom, that Germany could win the coming war. Diplomacy now became the servant of strategy. In a last flash of legality, the Germans wanted to document that somehow their resort to war was justified. Hence there must be a dispatch of ultimatums to Russia and France before an actual declaration of war, though not with any expectation that the ultimatums would be accepted. The ultimatum to Russia was easy: she was simply called upon to stop mobilising and to undo the steps already taken. Sazonov still did not understand that refusal of the German demand meant immediate war. He supposed only that the Germans would mobilise in their turn, and the Germans did not enlighten him, for fear that he might back down. Thus even on this last day of peace, 31st July, Sazonov thought only in terms of strong nerves and going nearer the edge. He explained that Russia's measures were merely precautionary. He was not to know that historians later, in their anxiety to exonerate Germany, would accept the German apology and accuse Sazonov of starting the war by taking defensive precautions.

The German approach to France was trickier still. The French had played no active part in the crisis — a modesty which was to be made an accusation against them by some historians later. There had been neither encouragement

Left: Temple of the god of war, the vast Krupp works at Essen.

nor restraint from Paris to St Petersburg. In France there had been nothing beyond preliminary measures without general mobilisation. The Germans would have been highly embarrassed if the French had answered that they had not mobilised and did not mean to do so. For the Germans had only a plan for defeating France and no other. The Germans had therefore made up their minds that, if the French returned a conciliatory answer, they would go on to demand the surrender of France's two frontier fortresses, Toul and Verdun, for the duration of the war, and this demand would surely provoke the French to a refusal. However, when the German ambassador presented the demand that France should promise not to mobilise, Viviani merely replied that she would consult her own interests. The Germans did not renew their demand. It occurred to them that France might agree, if only for a few days, and this would throw out Germany's offensive plans.

Germany declares war

However, by 1st August the Germans decided that their two ultimatums would not be accepted. The time had come for general mobilisation, which was in fact proclaimed before war was actually declared on France. Wilhelm II appreciated that this was the decisive act and made the most of it. Wearing full-dress Guards uniform he drove in an open carriage from Potsdam to the royal palace in Berlin, where he proposed to sign the order for general mobilisation before an audience of glittering generals. There was a bizarre interruption. Bethmann, who could attire himself only as a major, pushed through the dazzling throng. He brought the astonishing news that Sir Edward Grey had offered to stand surety for French neutrality. Wilhelm II reacted with optimistic excitement and declared that the preparations against France must be stopped. Moltke answered that this was impossible. It would involve the rerouting of 11,000 trains. He sulkily agreed to hold up movement over the western frontier for a few hours, and by then it turned out that Grey's message was a blunder or had been misunderstood. Grey now asserted that he had offered French and British neutrality only if Germany would refrain also from attacking Russia. More probably he had forgotten Russia as British statesmen often did and do.

Yet here again a slight change of time-table would have sent events quite a different way. Grey's offer was potential dynamite. The French were pledged by their alliance to attack Germany if Germany attacked Russia. Had the Germans assented quickly enough to Grey's proposal, France would have been compelled to appear as the aggressor. Or maybe not. For the Germans had no plan

100

for attacking Russia. If therefore they did not move in the west, there would be no war. And since the Russians had no offensive intentions, the war in the east would have been stuck also. These are idle speculations. Once the rulers of Germany decided that general mobilisation was their only means of safety, war had begun for all practical purposes.

On 1st August, failing a promise to stop mobilisation, Germany declared war on Russia. On 3rd August, Germany declared war on France on the quite unfounded pretext that French aviators had bombed Nuremberg. The bombs, if any, were dropped from German aeroplanes, or possibly there were no bombs at all. In an odd way, neither of these declarations was urgent. The Germans had no offensive plans against Russia, and therefore it was foolish of them to hurry the eastern war on. Nor had they offensive plans for attacking France directly. Their intention was to go through Belgium and to take the French armies in the rear. The ultimatum demanding free passage through Belgium for the German armies had been pulled out of a drawer by Moltke on 26th July and sent to Brussels. It was quite unsuited to the circumstances, containing a rigmarole of how French troops were preparing to invade Belgium. However, the pretext was of no importance. The ultimatum was delivered on the evening of 2nd August, actually twenty-four hours before the declaration of war against France which was supposed to justify it. By the time the Germans actually declared war on Belgium their troops were already on Belgian soil.

Between 28th July and 3rd August there were many decisions in the sense of answering the question: what shall we do or say next? But there was only one decision which turned the little Balkan conflict between Austria-Hungary and Serbia into a European war. That was the German decision to start general mobilisation on 31st July, and that was in its turn decisive because of the academic ingenuity with which Schlieffen, now in his grave, had attempted to solve the problem of a two-front war. One final step remained to be taken. The Germans had decided on a European war. It remained for the British to decide whether the war would spread beyond the Continent and become worldwide.

Left: Wilhelm II and the younger Moltke, chief of the German general staff, try to make sense of a map. The ingenuity with which the long-dead Schlieffen had tried to solve the problem of a two-front war had ensured that Germany must bring France into the struggle. A local conflict became a European war

101

Chapter 5
Decision in London

There was war between the two great alliances, as had long been expected. Two great powers settled their course on less precise terms. Italy was tied by contradictory promises, which in fact freed her from any embarrassing action. As a member of the Triple Alliance, she was pledged to support Germany in case of French aggression. She was also secretly pledged to France not to support Germany in an attack on France. She was pledged to remain neutral in a war between Russia and Austria-Hungary. On the other hand, she was pledged to join in if her Triple Alliance partners were at war with two other great powers. In all this, the Italians heard only the word neutrality. The Austrians for their part were determined not to have Italy as an ally.

Under such circumstances, it should have been easy for the Italians to follow a neutral and even a mediating path. But the Italians were also obsessed with the idea of compensation. They wanted to profit from action without taking it. It was too soon for them openly to abandon the Triple Alliance and to offer themselves to the other side. They therefore spent the entire crisis trying to extract from Vienna and Berlin statements of what rewards they would receive if they entered the war, which they had resolved not to do. Not surprisingly, their diplomacy proved barren. It had importance only as foreshadowing the search for rewards which finally brought Italy into the war in the following year.

The greatest decision in the crisis lay with the British government. It determined the future fate both of the British Empire and of Europe. For fifty years past, the British had followed a policy of detachment from continental affairs. Their relations with the continental powers, though intense and sometimes hostile, had been shaped by events outside Europe. There was one step which came near to a commitment. The British general staff had discussed with the French how their army could be used in case Great Britain entered a European war, and agreement had been reached. But there was no

Left: 'And this is the meaning of Empire Day.' (Chesterton)

103

pledge that the army would be used. There were those, particularly among the Conservatives, who would have liked a formal alliance with France. There were others, particularly among the Radicals, who thought that Anglo-French relations were already too close. The majority of politicians were reasonably content with Great Britain's equivocal position—half-in, half-out.

There was one striking difference between the way in which British policy was determined and how it happened elsewhere. On the continent the decision lay in the hands of individuals: the foreign minister, the ruler, and to some extent the chief-of-staff. In Austria-Hungary, it was Berchtold and Franz Joseph; in Russia, Sazonov and the Tsar; in Germany, Bethmann and Wilhelm II. The question hardly arose in France where there was no decision to make. But even here Viviani settled policy so far as there was one, with encouragement from Poincaré. If any of these foreign ministers had acted differently, the decisions would have been different. The councils of ministers, where they existed, were rarely informed and never consulted. For all practical purposes, they played no part in the crisis.

Grey tries to keep Great Britain out

In Great Britain decision lay with the Cabinet and beyond that with Parliament. Grey could not conduct an independent foreign policy even if he had wished to do so. He had to carry the Cabinet with him. Most of its members had little interest in European affairs. They expected Great Britain to stay out, the more so when the war seemed to originate in a remote Balkan struggle. In the first days, Grey agreed with them. He had no doubt that, whatever the rights and wrongs of the matter, it was Serbia's duty to give way. Some infringement of Serbian independence was better than a European war. He was prepared to mediate. He was not prepared to threaten. He did not warn Germany that Great Britain would go to war if Germany took the aggressive against France and Russia. He did not warn France, still less Russia, that Great Britain would remain neutral if they were unreasonable. He left both sides to make up their own minds. He pleaded later that the Cabinet would not have allowed him to do anything else. The truth is rather that he did not know what Great Britain would do or what course he himself would favour.

The British had one anxiety. They were pledged to maintain the neutrality of Belgium, and they regarded this as an essential British interest. Being good Liberals, they looked up what Gladstone had done at the outbreak of the Franco-German war in 1870 and carefully followed his precedent. On 31st July Grey therefore asked both

France and Germany for a promise to respect Belgian neutrality. The French at once gave the promise. The Germans answered that they could not reveal their plan of campaign. This was disturbing, though not in the way that was subsequently imagined. In the years immediately before the war Belgium had been more friendly with Germany than with France or Great Britain, and the British now feared that the Germans had struck a bargain which would allow them to pass through Belgium without resistance. On 1st August however the British received what they thought was good news. The Belgians declared that they were determined to defend their neutrality against all comers.

It is commonly supposed that many people foresaw the German invasion of Belgium. Some members of the British government, for instance, later claimed that they had not committed themselves to aiding France in the conviction that a German invasion of Belgium would remove all doubts. Even Grey wrote later: 'There was little for me to do. Circumstances and events were compelling decision.' Though it is always difficult, if not impossible, to prove a negative, this seems to be wisdom after the event. No affair illustrates better Maitland's dictum: 'It is important to remember that events now long in the past were once in the future.' The full-scale invasion of Belgium was inconceivable until it happened. British and French staff officers had discussed the defence of France. They had not discussed the defence of Belgium, and the military plans which they made were totally unsuited to it. The British staff officers concealed many things from the civilian politicians. But in this case they had nothing to conceal. They did not foresee the German invasion of Belgium and made no preparations against it.

It might be supposed that the French foresaw the invasion of Belgium and concealed this possibility in the hope that it would surprise the British into involvement. This, too, is not the case. The French military experts knew, of course, that the Germans had accumulated marshalling yards at Aachen and had greatly increased the railway lines from Aachen to the Belgian frontier. But they refused to believe that reservists, called to the colours after some years in civil life, could at once be used as fighting troops. They therefore much underestimated the forces available to the German high command on the western front and anticipated at most a German short-cut across Luxembourg. Joffre, the French commander-in-chief, had made dispositions to deal with this and indeed hoped that it would happen – he supposed that it would increase his chance of victory. There is clear proof of

Left: Great Britain, a patriotic demonstration by the young

French ignorance about the coming invasion of Belgium. In their desperate pleadings for British entry into the war, they used every conceivable argument, especially that of honourable commitment. It never occurred to them to argue that Belgium was in danger.

Great Britain seems safe

Thus, on 1st August, when the first declarations of war flashed across Europe, Great Britain still seemed to be well out of it. Almost half the Liberal Cabinet were against entering the war, and Grey himself did not propose it. Churchill, the most bellicose minister, sent a message to the Conservative leaders that the government was about to break up. He wanted preparations for an immediate coalition. Bonar Law, the Conservative leader, did not care for Churchill and returned no answer. Instead he sent a letter to Asquith the following day urging support for France and Russia. In the atmosphere of the moment, this letter seemed designed to embarrass the government rather than to produce any action.

When the Cabinet met on the morning of Sunday, 2nd August, Lord Morley, leader of the peace party, was cheerful and confident. He said to Churchill: 'Winston, we've beaten you after all.' Morley had thought of a policy which was both honourable and yet would avoid war. The French were constantly complaining that they had moved their fleet to the Mediterranean in the confident hope that the British would protect them in the Channel. Morley proposed to do so. The Germans should be warned that Great Britain could not allow the German fleet to enter the Channel and attack French shipping or French ports. In this way, the honourable undertaking to France would be discharged. Great Britain would be secured from a naval engagement on her doorstep. The way would be open for what Morley called 'diplomatic energy and armed neutrality', as against Grey's policy of armed intervention. The Cabinet accepted Morley's proposal. Later this looked like a first step towards supporting France, and its significance was therefore not grasped. At the time, it seemed a step the other way. The Germans, who had no intention of risking their fleet in the Channel, at once promised not to pass the straits of Dover. They attached a condition: Great Britain must remain neutral. The British did not accept this. All the same they were slipping into another honourable undertaking – this time with Germany.

Right: A peaceful society was plunged into war by its determination to honour a scrap of paper. *Bottom right:* The scrap of paper. *Top right:* Unbridled licence, mixed bathing at Weybridge in the summer of 1914. *Near right:* Bridled licence, church parade at Scarborough on the last weekend of the peace

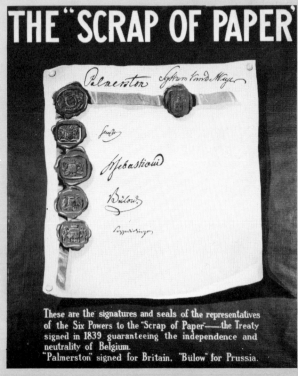

THE "SCRAP OF PAPER"

These are the signatures and seals of the representatives of the Six Powers to the "Scrap of Paper"—the Treaty signed in 1839 guaranteeing the independence and neutrality of Belgium.

"Palmerston" signed for Britain. "Bülow" for Prussia.

At 6.30 in the evening the British Cabinet met again. There were now reports, which proved true, that German troops were entering Luxembourg. British commitments to the neutrality of Luxembourg were vague and imprecise. They provided neither motive nor justification for action. But the German move raised the fear that they would also cross a corner of Belgium. What should Great Britain do then? Once more the Cabinet consulted the precedent of 1870. Gladstone's government had then resolved that 'a substantial violation of Belgian neutrality would compel us to take action'. The Cabinet of 2nd August 1914 repeated this resolution. Again, what appeared later as a step towards war was made as a security for peace. Crossing a corner of Belgium could be presented as not a substantial violation of her neutrality, and in fact, though the British did not know this, some Belgian ministers were playing with the idea of resisting the Germans only in the territory actually invaded, while keeping the rest of the country neutral.

These subtle calculations were made futile by what happened in Brussels exactly when the British Cabinet was meeting. The Belgians had mobilised on 1st August. They garrisoned their frontier against France as well as against Germany, and the people spent Sunday, 2nd August, in a holiday mood, happy that, as a small neutral, they would escape the clash of the great powers. At 6.30 pm the German minister sent a message that he wished to see the Foreign Minister. He arrived at 7 pm, pale and trembling. The Belgian said: 'Are you not well?' The German replied: 'I climbed the stairs too quickly.' He then read out the German demand to march through Belgium and asked for an answer within twelve hours. The paper dropped from his hands on to the floor. The Belgian said: 'No, no, it is not possible.'

The Belgian Cabinet met at 9 pm and sat until half-past two the following morning. They resolved to reject the German demand and to defend their neutrality. But they imagined that the Germans would hesitate if faced with a resolute resistance, still associated with neutrality. They supposed, too, as others did during the crisis, that there was plenty of time during which diplomacy could prevail. They did not therefore appeal to the other powers for assistance. On the contrary they ordered their troops to fire on any French soldiers crossing the frontier. The only appeal was from King Albert to King George for 'diplomatic assistance'.

The next morning, which was August Bank Holiday, the British Cabinet met again. It approved the draft of the speech which Grey was to make in the House of Commons that afternoon. One embarrassing point came out. Grey had told the French, but not the Germans, of the decision

taken the previous day to prevent the German fleet entering the Channel. Perhaps he had been hoping after all that the Germans would enter and so provoke a British intervention. Asquith had unwittingly spoilt Grey's manoeuvre by blurting out the story to the German ambassador during the evening. However, this was now all dead stuff. News of the German ultimatum to Belgium came in while the Cabinet was meeting. Morley felt that all was lost and resigned in despair. The rest of the Cabinet agreed that Grey should tack a passage about Belgium on to his existing draft. Lloyd George, who had been excited by the Bank Holiday crowds, was now as resolute as the rest.

'What happens now?'

In the afternoon Grey addressed the House of Commons. Most of his speech was a rambling defence of his past dealings with France. It was feeble and apologetic. He still made no recommendation and asked others to decide policy for him: 'Let every man look into his heart, and his own feelings, and construe the extent of his obligation for himself.' The MPs were disturbed and unhappy. Towards the end, Grey gave the news about Belgium, though still in a confused way. Opposition, though vocal, trailed away to nothing. Members departed, many of them dreaming that Belgium could be saved without war.

It almost seems that Grey shared this illusion. Churchill recounts that, as they left the House of Commons, he asked Grey: 'What happens now?' Grey replied: 'Now we shall send an ultimatum to Germany to stop the invasion of Belgium within twenty-four hours.' This sounds like a conversation made up after the event. At any rate nothing of the kind happened. The Cabinet met during the evening and resolved to ask the Germans for an assurance that they would respect Belgian neutrality. There was no threat of war, no time limit. No decision actually to go to war was ever made by the British Cabinet.

Grey still thought that there was no hurry – or perhaps it was another case of circumstances deciding for him. After the Cabinet he had dinner and went to bed. The polite request to Germany was not sent off until 9.30 the next morning. By then it was already out of date. The first German troops had crossed the Belgian frontier at 8 am. News reports of this reached London about midday. There was still no Belgian appeal for assistance. (This reached London only at 12.50 am on 5th August, almost two hours after Great Britain had declared war on Germany.) Grey did not again consult the Cabinet. He may have consulted

Left: French civilians greet the first members of the British Expeditionary Force to arrive for the defence of their country – just in time to join in a general retreat before the Germans

Asquith. The King was not informed. Essentially Grey acted on his own.

At 2 pm on 4th August he dispatched an ultimatum to Germany. The Germans were again asked for an assurance that they would respect the neutrality of Belgium. A satisfactory reply must be received 'here by 12 o'clock tonight'. The request was of course refused. Goschen, the British ambassador, saw Bethmann at 7 pm. Bethmann said that England was going to war 'just for a scrap of paper'.

Did he use these very words? We shall never know, for when anyone thought of asking both Bethmann and Goschen were dead. We do not know whether Bethmann spoke in German or in English—probably in German. We know, however, that the words were already running in Goschen's mind. A fortnight earlier there had been private theatricals at the British embassy. The play was a piece by Sardou, its title: *A Scrap of Paper*. Goschen burst into tears and asked for his passports.

'It's all up'

In London Asquith told the House of Commons that an ultimatum had been sent. He went to his private room where his wife asked him: 'So it is all up?' He replied: 'Yes, it's all up' and also burst into tears. Yet apparently British ministers were still not sure that all was up. Asquith, Grey, Lloyd George, and others met in the Cabinet Room, waiting for the reply from Germany which never came. Someone had a bright idea for shortening the suspense. Germany had Central European Time, which was one hour later than Greenwich Time (then unsullied by the later invention of Summer Time). Midnight in Berlin was therefore 11 pm in London, and the British ultimatum could be treated as expiring at that hour. This did not accord with the wording of the ultimatum which had asked for an answer *here,* that is London, by midnight. Was someone afraid that the Germans might give a favourable answer after all? Was it an ingenious idea for getting off to bed? Or was it merely another example of the unreasoning haste which characterised the entire crisis? We shall never know.

At 10.15 pm the King held a privy council at Buckingham Palace. It was attended by the First Commissioner of Works and two court officials. The Privy Council authorised a state of war with Germany from 11 pm. This was the formality which took Great Britain into war. With a last flash of muddle the wrong declaration of war was sent to the German ambassador. A news agency reported that Germany had declared war on Great Britain. A counter declaration was at once sent to the German ambassador. The news then turned out to be false. A Foreign Office

clerk raced round to the German embassy and recovered the British note which the ambassador had not opened. The clerk substituted the correct declaration which merely asserted that Germany had not replied. It was then 11.5 pm. At exactly the same time Churchill left the Cabinet Room for the Admiralty and dispatched the telegram to all warships: 'Commence hostilities against Germany.'

It was easy for the Royal Navy to do this in theory, though, given the shortage of German ships out of port, not so easy in practice. But what else should the British do? Every other country had had detailed war plans drawn up before the diplomacy began, and the war plans made the running. But the British resolved on war first and decided on action afterwards. The Cabinet had authorised the mobilisation of the expeditionary force on 3rd August. They had not decided where it should go to, if anywhere. On 5th August Asquith, who was acting secretary of state for war, summoned a war council. The civilians present were Grey, Haldane, and Churchill; the soldiers, every distinguished general Asquith could lay his hands on.

There was a rambling and uninformed discussion. Great Britain had gone to war for the sake of Belgian neutrality. How was she to ensure this? Lord Roberts, the senior general present, suggested that the expeditionary force should go to Antwerp. Churchill answered that the navy could not guarantee a safe passage east of the Straits of Dover. Sir John French, who was to command the expeditionary force, thought that the army might cross the Channel to Le Havre and then decide where to go – perhaps to Antwerp, perhaps to Amiens. Sir Douglas Haig thought that the regular soldiers should stop at home and train the mass armies of the future. Sir Henry Wilson, director of military operations, cut in impatiently. He explained that there was no choice. The expeditionary force could not help the Belgians. It could only take its allotted place on the French left wing. The marshalling yards were prepared, trucks ready, lines cleared. It was Maubeuge or nowhere.

On 6th August the Cabinet resolved that the expeditionary force should go to Amiens. No one took any notice. The time-table said Maubeuge. To Maubeuge it went. In this accidental way Great Britain found herself involved as a continental power in a continental war.

Left: A German cartoonist attacks the two 'war criminals' who had forced his country into war; Grey (top), whom the Germans blamed for Great Britain's involvement, and Princip (bottom)

Chapter 6
The End of the Line

On the last day of July 1914 the international expresses
stopped running all over Europe. They were not to run
again for six years and never in their old untrammelled
glory. Troop trains ran instead. By 4th August the
great powers of Europe, other than Italy, were at war.
However not all were at war with each other. France,
Germany, Russia, and Great Britain had become involved in war because of a quarrel which was initially
Austrian. Yet when the others were at war with each
other, Austria-Hungary, the cause of it all, was still
at war with no country except Serbia. Berchtold continued to hope that something would turn up. Even after
the German mobilisation, he went on talking about a
diplomatic solution. When the Germans declared war on
Russia, Berchtold used this as a further excuse for
delay: Austria-Hungary was pledged to aid Germany
only if Russia attacked Germany and not the other way
round. Conrad for his part thought that every day without a declaration of war made his precious plans for
mobilisation easier. The Germans lost patience. They
were at war for Austria-Hungary's sake, and yet she
took no action even on paper.

Finally on 6th August Berchtold dispatched a declaration of war to St Petersburg, alleging quite untruly that
Russia had seen fit 'to open hostilities against Germany'.
There was now an awkward pause on the other side.
Neither France nor Great Britain desired to go to war
against Austria-Hungary, nor had they any practical
means of doing so except for naval blockade in the
Adriatic. Once Austria-Hungary declared war on Russia,
France was technically bound to go to war by the terms of
the Franco-Russian alliance. But French statesmen did
not wish to invoke the alliance for the sake of left-wing
opinion; and British statesmen, of course, were even less
attracted to this obligation. The French therefore invented the story that Austrian troops had been sent to the
western front, and on this pretext declared war against
Austria-Hungary on 12th August. The British govern-

Left: Young recruits demonstrate outside the War Office

113

ment added its own declaration of war at once, merely because the French had already done so. Both British and French diplomats still asserted their friendship towards Austria-Hungary. Little did they foresee that before the war ended the dismemberment of Austria-Hungary would become a principal Allied war aim. To round off the record, Austria-Hungary declared war against Belgium on 29th August, alleging, again untruthfully, that Belgium was 'lending her military co-operation to France and Great Britain'.

Luxembourg did not go to war despite Germany's violation of her territory. Rumania did not go to war despite the binding terms of her alliance with Austria-Hungary and Germany. Montenegro went to war against Austria-Hungary in support of Serbia, even though Prince Nicholas knew that he would lose his throne if the Serbs won and equally, of course, if they lost. The insatiable appetite of his people for war gave him no choice. The Turks could have chosen neutrality as they did in the Second World War. Instead, with gratuitous folly and misjudgement, they committed themselves to alliance with Germany and thus provided the Entente with another ancient empire to dismember. Portugal wished to honour her alliance with Great Britain. Being forbidden to do so by the British, she contented herself with not declaring neutrality. The Japanese also honoured their alliance with Great Britain, though much to their own advantage. They demanded German withdrawal from Far Eastern waters and the surrender of Germany's leased territory of Kiao-Chow. The Germans did not reply, and Japan declared war on 23rd August. All other powers remained neutral, some with good intent, some for the duration of the war.

None of the cherished plans provided the quick and final victory for which they had been designed. The French plans came near to producing catastrophe — for the French, not for the Germans. The French armies were mobilised with great efficiency on the German frontier. They were then sent forward against the most heavily fortified positions in the German line. There was no attempt at strategy or tactical deployment. These were among **118** ▷

Right: Count von Schlieffen, his dead finger was on the button.
*Far right: The original plan **(top)** which dictated the thinking of the German general staff for more than twenty years. When the younger Moltke came to use it in 1914 **(centre)** he failed to appreciate the essence of the plan. His armies swung east of Paris to finish off the French and so exposed a flank to attack by the Paris garrison. The railway network on Germany's western border **(bottom)** shows the bunching of lines at Aachen which forced the Germans to feed their troops through the junction and over the border as soon as their mobilisation got under way*

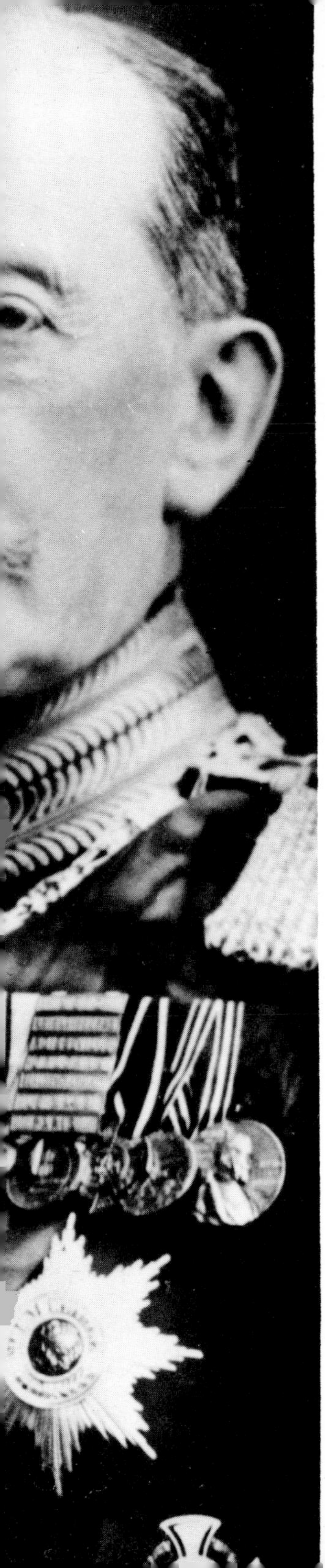

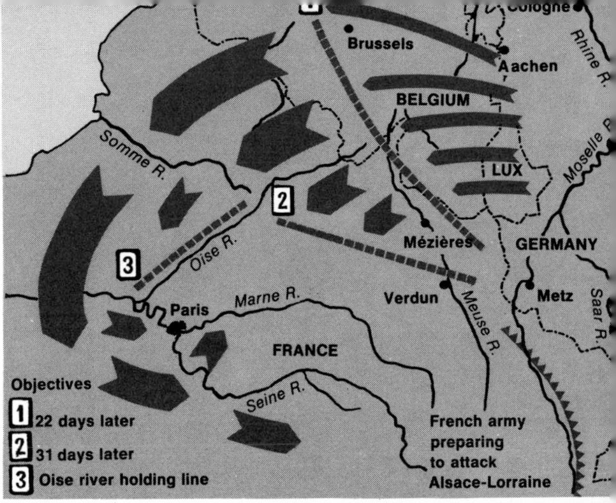
Cologne
Brussels
Aachen
Rhine R.
BELGIUM
Moselle R.
Somme R.
LUX
2
GERMANY
Mézières
3
Oise R.
Metz
Paris
Marne R.
Verdun
Saar R.
Meuse R.
FRANCE
Seine R.
Objectives
1 22 days later
2 31 days later
3 Oise river holding line
French army
preparing
to attack
Alsace-Lorraine

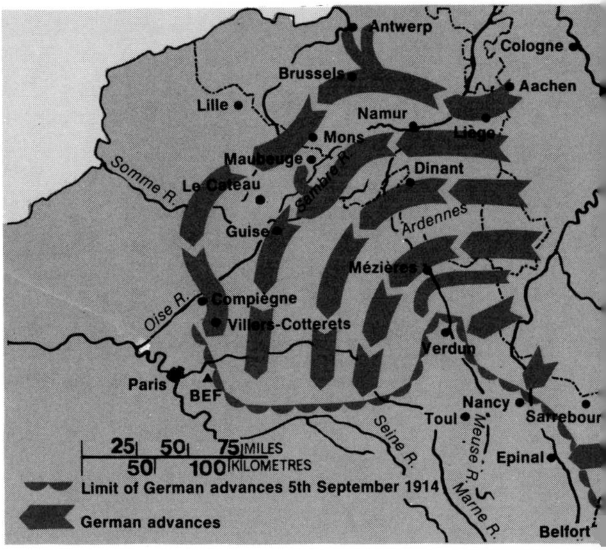
Antwerp
Cologne
Brussels
Aachen
Lille
Namur
Liège
Mons
Maubeuge
Sambre R.
Dinant
Somme R.
Le Cateau
Ardennes
Guise
Mézières
Oise R.
Compiègne
Villers-Cotterets
Verdun
Paris
BEF
Nancy
Toul
Sarrebour
Seine R.
Meuse R.
25 50 75 MILES
50 100 KILOMETRES
Epinal
Limit of German advances 5th September 1914
Marne R.
German advances
Belfort

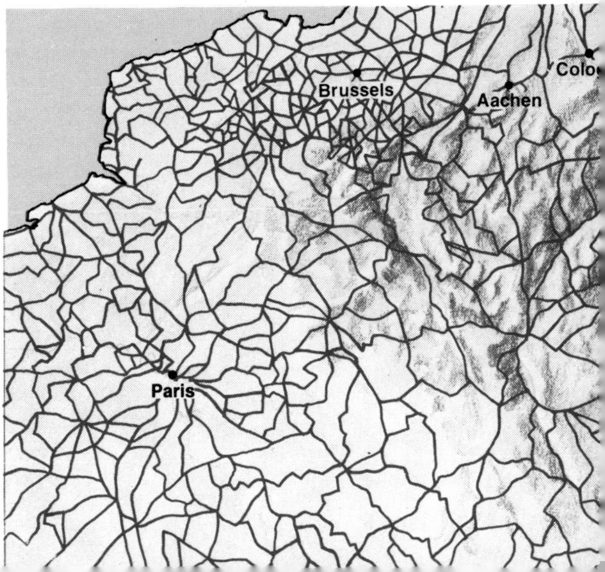
Brussels
Aachen
Paris

The happiness
of a world gone mad

So the time-tables triumphed. All over Europe men marched off to begin the journeys which would not end until they triumphantly reached their enemy's capital. In every country men had been told that these great untried armies and the plans, prepared in such remote theory, were sure to triumph when put to the test. Every nation was composed of warriors. Every general was a genius. Victory was certain. The war would be decided in one great battle, and all would be over by Christmas. But never have time-tables been so tragically inaccurate. For the men who went to war there was no glorious victory, only wounds, death, or, at best, more than four years of suffering in the trenches. In the first days of enthusiasm the soldiers laughed and joked, scribbled light-hearted messages with chalk on their railway carriages and waved to the pretty girls. **Right:** French troops set off for Berlin. **Below:** German troops start for Paris

1914: unknown.

the worst, though least known, massacres of the First World War. Ironically, the French armies were saved from total destruction by the Schlieffen plan. The development of the German threat to the French left wing finally compelled Joffre to break off his senseless attacks in Lorraine. Instead, much against his will, he won the battle of the Marne.

The German advance through Belgium and into northern France was the most perfect operation of military art as this was understood in the early 20th century. The German armies moved with almost effortless precision. The time-tables proved accurate to the minute even when the Germans were on enemy territory. Decisive victory was not achieved. The German impetus was running down even before it encountered resolute resistance. When the German troops had to face real fighting, they had been on the march for nearly a month — often covering 40 miles a day. This sort of physical exhaustion was a problem which Schlieffen had not allowed for. His marvellous plan broke down for two reasons. French armies, directed by Joffre, stood immediately in the way. French armies, directed by Galliéni, threatened the German right flank. The manoeuvre had failed. As was the rule in manoeuvres, it was then abandoned.

The British deployment on the French left wing was also beautifully conducted. The expeditionary force duly arrived at Maubeuge. Instead of settling into a quiet sector of the French line, it found itself full in the track of the German army which was sweeping across Belgium. The British were rudely pushed aside. Then later they played their part, somewhat cautiously, in the battle of the Marne. But the British forces were now embedded in the French front. A landing in the German rear might have been more effective. Perhaps Morley's 'armed neutrality' could have had a more decisive effect, once Germans and French had fought each other to a standstill. There had, of course, been another British mobilisation. The Grand Fleet assembled at Scapa Flow. No Armageddon followed. On the contrary, the periscope of a mythical German submarine led the Grand Fleet to abandon Scapa Flow and to seek refuge in the remote bays of western Ireland. For many months, Great Britain and the Channel were defended only by the shadow of Nelson's name. This proved effective.

The great powers had plunged into war for the sake of quick victory. They continued to pursue this illusive hope for the next four years. Afterwards men looked back and puzzled how it could have happened, as they continue to do to the present day. There was a varied array of war criminals. The Allies wished to arraign 'Kaiser Bill'. This was ironically perverse. As the record shows, Wil-

helm II was one of the few who made persistent and constructive attempts to avoid war. Bethmann had greater responsibility, yet came off far better. Poor Tsar Nicholas also received much condemnation, partly because he had been conveniently murdered by the Bolsheviks. Yet it seems that if the affair had been left to the crowned heads of Europe there would never have been war at all. The so-called 'military monarchs' were peaceful, well-meaning men. Unfortunately, in the 20th century, they believed it their duty to do what their statesmen said.

No popular demand for war
Some have propounded an exactly opposite explanation. The war has been blamed on the peoples of Europe. The cheering crowds, it is said, gave the statesmen no choice and drove them into war. This, too, will not do. The crowds cheered only after the decisions had been made. There were none of the demonstrations, intended to make statesmen do something or not do something, that there were later in the 1930s and often are at the present day. In Austria-Hungary, for instance, the crowds cried 'Death to the Serbian dogs' only after war had been declared. No one in Berlin waved banners inscribed 'Stand by Austria-Hungary'. Indeed this was a sentiment which would have occurred to no German outside the diplomatic service. The German crowds cheered only when mobilisation was proclaimed, and they did so because they believed that Germany was in imminent danger of a great Russian invasion.

In St Petersburg there were no banners inscribed 'Stand by Serbia'. Here, too, the crowds cheered only when Tsar Nicholas II took a solemn oath not to make peace as long as there was a single invader on Russian soil — though as a matter of fact there were none at the time. French crowds demonstrated patriotic support for President Poincaré when he returned from St Petersburg, but it would be absurd to suppose that he needed this encouragement. British crowds were the only ones which demonstrated before their country was at war. The Bank Holiday crowds would have been puzzled to say what they were cheering for. Few Englishmen cared about France. None cared about Russia, and few knew much about Belgium. Presumably English people felt that, when other countries were already at war, their own should not be left out. It would be unfair to deduce from this that the English were peculiarly bellicose. Nor did their cheers have much influence on the decisions of the government.

In every country the governments decided, almost

Left: Italian armed neutrality, the delinquent member of the Triple Alliance found it a most uncomfortable experience

without weighing public opinion. More narrowly, foreign ministers decided as a sort of technical exercise. The considerations which moved them were no different from those on previous occasions. It has been suggested that the balance of power had broken down. Hence the German ministers were eager for war. This is the reverse of the truth. For years past, Germany had been the strongest of the powers, and others – Russia in 1909, France in 1905 and 1911 – had given way when faced with a German threat. In 1914 the French and, more hesitantly, the Russians believed that they were strong enough to face the threat. This may have been a mere change of sentiment or it may have been a real change of power. The actual outcome certainly showed that Germany could not win a quick victory as everyone had expected her to do during earlier crises.

These earlier crises had ended without war, partly because the issues at stake were not worth fighting about. French access to the upper Nile in 1898; French control of Morocco in 1905 and 1911; even Serbia's claim to Bosnia in 1909 were topics of remote importance. There was a topic of real importance in 1914: the assertion of Habsburg prestige against Serb nationalism. But none of the great powers wished to dispute this. All would have acquiesced in the Halt in Belgrade, a perfectly satisfactory diplomatic solution. Instead the crisis ran away with them.

When cut down to essentials, the sole cause for the outbreak of war in 1914 was the Schlieffen plan – product of the belief in speed and the offensive. Diplomacy functioned until the German demand that France and Russia should not mobilise. No power could have accepted such a demand in the circumstances of the age. Yet the Germans had no deliberate aim of subverting the liberties of Europe. No one had time for a deliberate aim or time to think. All were trapped by the ingenuity of their military preparations, the Germans most of all. In every country, the peoples imagined that they were being called to a defensive war, and in a sense they were right. Since every general staff believed that attack was the only form of defence, every defensive operation appeared as an attack to someone else.

There is no mystery about the outbreak of the First World War. The deterrent failed to deter. This was to be expected sooner or later. A deterrent may work ninety-nine times out of a hundred. On the hundredth occasion it produces catastrophe. There is a contemporary moral here for those who like to find one.

Left: The triumph of the time-tables, the men go forth to war

Chronology of Events

1870-1 Franco-Prussian War
1875 Rebellion in Bosnia against Turkish rule
1878 Congress of Berlin transfers administration of Bosnia and Herzegovina to Austria-Hungary
1879 Bismarck begins German alliance with Austria-Hungary
1882 Italy is added to the Austro-German alliance, forming the Triple Alliance
1884 Berlin Conference on African affairs provides for free trade in the Congo Basin and the abolition of the slave trade; the Congo Free State is recognised
1893 Franco-British crisis over Siam
1894 France and Russia form the Dual Alliance
1898 Kitchener confronts Marchand at Fashoda. First German Navy Bill passed, and Tirpitz founds Navy League
1899 The French renounce all territory along the Nile

1902 The Anglo-Japanese Alliance. Triple Alliance renewed
1904 The Entente Cordiale settles Anglo-French differences
1905 First Moroccan crisis when Kaiser Wilhelm visits Tangier. Anglo-French military conversations
1906 The Algeciras Act gives France and Spain chief control in Morocco
1907 The Anglo-Russian Convention on Persia, Afghanistan, and Tibet
1908 Austria annexes Bosnia and Herzegovina
1909 Serbia yields to Austria in the Bosnian dispute
1911 Second Moroccan crisis: the German gunboat *Panther* arrives at Agadir
1912 The Sultan of Morocco signs a treaty making Morocco a French protectorate
18th October: outbreak of the First Balkan War
1913 **29th June-30th July:** Second Balkan War

1914 **28th June:** Archduke Franz Ferdinand and his wife are assassinated by Gavrilo Princip at Sarajevo
5th July: the Austrian ambassador discusses the situation with Kaiser Wilhelm II
23rd July: Austria-Hungary delivers her ultimatum to Belgrade
24th July: Sazonov, Russian foreign minister, urges mobilisation in military districts adjacent to Austria-Hungary
25th July: Serbia mobilises and moves government to Niš. 5.55 pm: Pašić delivers Serbia's reply and Austria-Hungary breaks off relations
26th July: Sir Edward Grey proposes four-power mediation of the Balkan crisis; Sazonov seeks talks with Austria-Hungary
28th July: Austria-Hungary declares war on Serbia. The 'Halt in Belgrade' is proposed by the Kaiser
30th July: Russia mobilises
1st August: Germany declares war on Russia. Belgium declares her neutrality and mobilises
2nd August: Germany sends an ultimatum to Belgium
3rd August: Germany declares war on France and invades Belgium
4th August: Great Britain and Belgium declare war on Germany; Germany declares war on Belgium
5th August: Asquith summons a war council
6th August: the BEF goes to Maubeuge. Austria-Hungary declares war on Russia. Serbia declares war on Germany
12th August: France and Great Britain declare war on Austria-Hungary

Top: Tsar Nicholas II (left), Admiral Sir John Fisher (centre) the Congress of Berlin 1878 (right). Middle: Cabrinović (left) and Princip (right), 'War is a part of God's creation' a German match-box cover (right). Bottom: The first reservists are called up in Berlin (left and centre), a lonely French pacifist makes his protest in 1913 (right)

Index of main people and places

Author's suggestions for further reading

After 1919 the study of war origins became a large-scale industry. The Germans were out to show that they were not solely responsible for the war, as alleged in the Treaty of Versailles. Many English and American scholars came to agree with them, in a perverse Anglo-Saxon way. The actual course of events seemed too childishly simple, and the explanations disappointingly crude. It was expected that, if more were known, more would be found out — an expression of the usual modern illusion that knowledge leads to understanding. The statesmen wrote their memoirs. The foreign ministries opened their archives or rather allowed scholars of high repute to publish selections from them. Entire books have been manufactured out of the bibliography of war origins. A short cut is to turn to the bibliography in A.J.P.Taylor, *The Struggle for Mastery in Europe 1848-1918* (1954).

Of secondary works, the most preposterously pro-German is Harry Elmer Barnes, *The Genesis of the War* (1926); the more adroitly pro-German, S.B.Fay, *The Origins of the World War* (1929); and the most sensible, B.E.Schmitt, *The Coming of the War* (1930). All were written a long time ago. An Italian journalist, Luigi Albertini, produced an even more thorough and slightly later study, *The Origins of the War of 1914*, translated into English (1952-57). It was the last of the old-fashioned treatments.

Recently, there has been a new start with the advantage of greater perspective and greater access to archives. Vladimir Dedijer, *The Road to Sarajevo* (1966), provides a fascinating analysis which supersedes all previous accounts, particularly as these were all written from a pro-Austrian point of view. Gerhard Ritter edited *The Schlieffen Plan* (1958). Fritz Fischer, in *Griff nach der Weltmacht* (1961), has displayed Germany's aims during the war and has argued that she possessed these aims before war broke out. I.Geiss has reinforced this argument in a collection of documents, entitled *July 1914* (1967). It is more likely that German statesmen, like others, did not know what they were doing. A good popular account of the critical period is George Malcolm Thomson, *The Twelve Days* (1964).

Only now are the archives being opened without restrictions, or with few. It is hard to surmise what will be found out — if anything. It is my impression that the policies of Berchtold and Bethmann, Sazonov and Poincaré are as fully illuminated as they are ever likely to be. But there remain plenty of surprises in the study of British policy. We still do not know in detail what happened inside the Cabinet, nor what judgements were given by the military experts. These are rewarding topics for investigation.

AJPTaylor, Editor-in-Chief of Purnell's *History of the 20th Century,* is Fellow of Magdalen College, Oxford, and is also in charge of the Beaverbrook Library. His books include: *Bismarck, The Habsburg Monarchy, The Course of German History, The First World War, The Origins of the Second World War, The Troublemakers,* and *English History 1914-1945* (part of the Oxford History of England).

JMRoberts, General Editor of the Macdonald *Library of the 20th Century,* is Fellow and Tutor in Modern History at Merton College, Oxford. He is also General Editor of Purnell's *History of the 20th Century,* Joint-Editor of the *English Historical Review,* and author of *Europe 1880-1945* in the Longmans History of Europe. He has been English Editor of the *Larousse Encyclopaedia of Modern History,* has reviewed for *The Observer, New Statesman,* and *Spectator,* and given regular talks on the BBC.

Library of the 20th Century

Publisher: John Selwyn Gummer
Editor: Christopher Falkus
Executive Editor: Jonathan Martin
Editorial Assistant: Jenny Ashby
Designed by: Brian Mayers/ Germano Facetti
Assistant Designer: Ken Carroll
Research: Georgina Barker

Pictures selected from the following sources

Belgrade Military Museum 38 56 57
Bibliothèque Nationale, Paris 6 14 53 112
Central Press, City Museum, Belgrade 55
Kenneth Griffith Collection 17
Harlingue-Viollet 11
Heeresgeschichtliches Museum, Vienna 24 53 66
Historia-Photo, Bad Sachsa 68
Imperial War Museum 118
London Museum 36 104
Mons Museum 118
Moro, Rome 68
Musée de la Guerre 91
Musée des Arts Décoratifs 36 91
Musée Royal de l'Armée, Brussels 110
National Army Museum, Sandhurst 17
Nationalbibliothek Bildarchiv, Vienna 8 50
Novosti Press Agency 12 13 68 78 81 83
Radio Times Hulton Picture Library 30 70 107
Editions Rencontre, Lausanne 30 76
Rockefeller Collection, New York 34
Roger Viollet 98 114 115
Snark 33 120
Staatsbibliothek, Berlin 84 116
Südd-Verlag, Munich Endpaper 2 22 30 42 64 95 97
Paul Tabori 48 62
Tasiemka 8 11 73
Oscar Tellgmann 21
Ullstein 37 46 59 60 90 100
John Wood, Caligari 92

The extract on page 16 is from *Liaison 1914* (2nd edition 1966) by E.L.Spears. It is reproduced by kind permission of the author